Violence and nationalist politics in Derry City, 1920–1923

Maynooth Studies in Local History

SERIES EDITOR Raymond Gillespie

This is one of the six titles to be published in the Maynooth Studies in Local History series in 2003. With these six the series will now comprise of over fifty volumes. The majority of these have their origins as theses completed for the M.A. in Local History course in NUI Maynooth that is itself ten years old. This achievement is evidence of the enthusiasm for the study of local history in Ireland but it also reflects the importance attached to local developments in the writing of the story of the Irish past in a new millennium. These volumes are also testimony to a growing methodological sophistication in the writing of Irish local history in the last ten years. Like many of their predecessors they employ the analytical framework of community in trying to understand local developments in the past. In a rapidly changing society 'community' has resonances of an idyllic society characterized by mutual support and a sense belonging held in tension with insularity and remoteness. As such the idea can conceal tensions and differences in such imagined worlds. Yet these local studies resist the tendency to such stereotyping. With their predecessors they reveal something of the realities of the workings of local communities in the changing world of the past. Individuals belonged to many communities in the past and such memberships were often fluid and determined by a variety of motives, agendas and external forces. Whether the community was that of the landed estate, local town, large city, political party or gentry world, its membership was continually fluctuating and those who belonged to these diverse communities were rarely of the same mind as each other. Social, religious and political divisions were all realities in these local worlds of the past, yet those who were often at odds with each other at least agreed on the basic rules for the debate, albeit sometimes the rules of violence or resistance. Countering the centrifugal forces often threatening to tear local societies apart, there were equally powerful centripetal tendencies holding it together. The way in which these forces combined created the local distinctiveness, or 'personality', of the local regions of Ireland. These studies, like their predecessors, contribute to an understanding of that process, and together they are remaking our understanding of modern Ireland.

Maynooth Studies in Local History: Number 52

Violence and nationalist politics in Derry City, 1920–1923

Ronan Gallagher

FOUR COURTS PRESS

Set in 10pt on 12pt Bembo by
Carrigboy Typesetting Services, Co. Cork for
FOUR COURTS PRESS LTD
7 Malpas Street, Dublin 8, Ireland
e-mail: info@four-courts-press.ie
http://www.four-courts-press.ie
and in North America for
FOUR COURTS PRESS
c/o ISBS, 920 N.E. 58th Avenue, Suite 300, Portland, OR 97213.

ISBN 1–85182–760–9

Printed in Ireland by
ßetaprint Ltd, Dublin

Contents

Acknowledgements

First and foremost I would like to thank my wife Alison for all her help, encouragement and advice, while I researched, wrote, and completed this work. This book was born as a Master's thesis in the history department of St Patrick's College, Drumcondra, Dublin, in September 2000. I owe a great debt to all the teaching staff in the department, but in particular to my supervisor, Dr Diarmaid Ferriter, and head of history, Dr James Kelly. There are many libraries and archival departments that facilitated my study over a period of time that I would also like to remember: Heritage & Museum Services, Derry City Council; editorial office of the *Derry Journal*; National Library of Ireland; National Archives; Military Archives; Public Record Office, Belfast; University College Dublin, Archives; and the library staff of St Patrick's College. Additionally, I would like to remember the following individuals who were gracious in their assistance and time: Joost Augusteijn, Manus Bradley, Frank Curran, Richard Doherty, Sarah Gearty, Brian Hanley, Mary Gallagher, Brian Lacey, Siobhán McEleney, Eamon Phoenix and Dermot Francis, who died in May 2002. I would also like to thank the following regarding reproduction rights: the Library, Magee College, University of Ulster, for their permission to use the photograph on the cover; and Ronnie O'Doherty, Buncrana, Co. Donegal, for the photograph of Hugh C. O'Doherty, which was taken from *The making of a minority: political developments in Derry and the North, 1912–25* (Derry, 1997) by Colm Fox. In conclusion, I would like to thank Dr Raymond Gillespie of the Modern History department at NUI Maynooth who has given this text a home.

1. Background: setting the scene for 1920

In his recent book, journalist Ed Moloney, when writing about gerrymandering and unionist domination in 1920s Derry, neglects to tell the reader that Londonderry corporation was controlled, for three years, by a nationalist/Sinn Féin majority from 1920 to 1923.[1] To a younger age group, the prominence of nationalist politicians in the city at that time probably comes as something of a surprise, but to an ever-dwindling older generation who either had first-hand experience or heard their parents speak of the period, this knowledge is nothing new. But how did such a traditionally unionist-dominated city, with its great 16th-century walls built to protect its protestant population from the Irish natives, change utterly by the early part of the 20th century?

Derry developed rapidly throughout the 19th century. Industrial life galvanized the city, giving rise to an ever-increasing catholic population. Distilleries, bacon-curing, flax mills, shipbuilding, transatlantic sailing, foundries and the great shirt industry all helped to expand the local industrial base. The development of the shirt industry in particular was of paramount importance, as factory owners were not bothered whether their profits accrued via the hands of a catholic or a protestant worker: the profits at the end of the day were what mattered. This economic expansion was partly fuelled by immigrant workers from Donegal and Tyrone, many of whom had suffered due to successive potato crop failures and had moved to the city as a result.[2] With money, catholic self-belief grew in tandem with political developments, culminating with the gradual build-up of the catholic population outside the city walls. In 1889, the *Londonderry Guardian* remarked: 'the character of the population has undergone a material change in late years, large numbers of the Celtic race having immigrated into the city and found employment as labourers and in other capacities'.[3] The census of that year shows a figure of 13,821 catholics against 11,421 for all other denominations.[4] When Vesey Knox, a local protestant solicitor, was elected as a Parnellite MP, in the general election of July 1895, the signs were that in a subtle, but nevertheless pronounced, way, change was occurring in the city's politics.[5] But successive schemes, which became known as gerrymandering, curtailed the political power that nationalists could wield, despite their numerical superiority. By rigging electoral boundaries to keep catholics in the one place, legislation kept protestants firmly in the ascendancy until the 1970s. The exception to this was 1920–3. As Frank Curran noted: 'the manoeuvre [Londonderry Improvement bill of 1896] was the first gerrymander of Derry, and repetitions in 1919, 1922 and 1936 enabled Unionists to defeat mathematics and retain local government control of Derry'.[6]

With home rule changing the political climate, Derry became the central focus for both nationalism and unionism in 1913. In this year nine counties of Ulster returned to Westminster a majority of 17 to 16 MPs in favour of home rule. A by-election on 30 January for the Derry seat saw a local shirt manufacturer and protestant, David Cleghorn Hogg (at the time, lord lieutenant of Co. Londonderry), elected on the home rule ticket. It is debatable whether or not he gave a commitment to the pursuit of home rule, but nevertheless, nationalist votes ensured his success.[7] Indeed, it has been argued that another protestant liberal, William Tillie, would have been a better candidate since Hogg was then in his mid-70s (he died in 1914).[8] During the election, the influence of the local clergy was vital. By supporting a protestant candidate for the home rule movement, they were able to demonstrate their tolerance to the national and British press when it came to religious and political accommodation in the city. It was almost the pinnacle of their power, as society would dramatically change over the next seven years. As Desmond Murphy noted:

> Hogg's narrow victory over Colonel Pakenham demonstrated conclusively the power of the catholic clergy to dictate politics but ironically their moment of greatest success presaged a period in which their authority would come under its most serious challenge since the mid-1860s.[9]

Ulster at the time was an unstable society where civil war seemed inevitable. With the establishment of rival military organizations (Ulster Volunteer Force and the National Volunteers), both sides seemed set on a collision course before the First World War broke out in 1914. With the backing of the Irish Parliamentary party (IPP), Westminster temporarily shelved home rule.

Although Sinn Féin had established clubs nationwide, it was still relatively weak in Derry, thanks to the influence of Bishop McHugh and his clergy, all of whom gave their support to the IPP. The party organized itself nationally under the umbrella of the United Irish League, which was responsible for electioneering while acting as a platform for the views and policies of the leadership. But the IPP's political base was eroded between 1914 and 1916 on two fronts: firstly, subventions from the United Irish League of America dried up when the leader of the IPP, John Redmond, urged his followers to join the British army after the outbreak of war in Europe; and secondly, support in Ulster was eroded when Redmond agreed to the partition of the country in 1916 at the behest of Lloyd George;[10] whereas the former hit IPP support nationally, in Ulster, the 'evil' of partition was what incensed nationalists and the clergy in particular. As early as July 1916 Bishop McHugh abandoned his

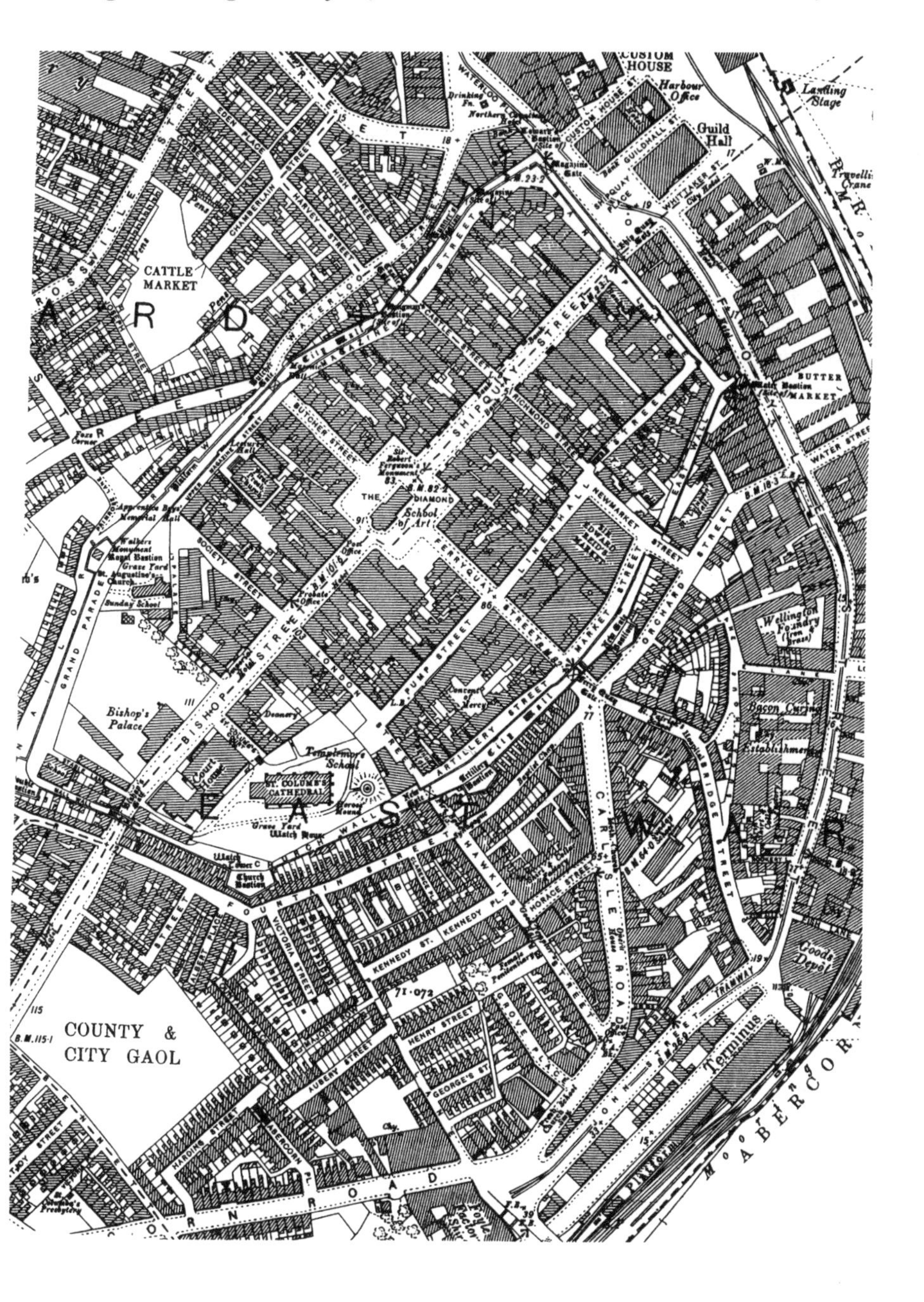

1 Derry city, taken from a 1904 map, showing some of the streets mentioned in the text

support for Redmond to seek a more satisfactory solution to the threat of partition.[11]

The war gave the local economy a much-needed boost, but stagnation returned once it ended in 1918. This had a marked impact on the political situation in the city. Originally, the rise of advanced nationalist thinking had been stemmed as a result of the war. In Derry, Bishop McHugh had supported the call to arms and, along with his priests, encouraged the men of the city to fight for Britain, as the cause of catholic Belgium and the implementation of home rule were justifiable reasons to volunteer.[12] But as Redmond sank deeper into the mire of partition for Ulster and 'physical force nationalism' received a badly needed boost with the events of Easter week, 1916, the scene in Derry slowly changed. Rising casualty lists from the war also damaged Redmond's cause. First, the Gaelic Athletic Association (GAA) and the Gaelic Literary Society were re-established by Derry Republicans who had been released from prison in the aftermath of 1916. The city's first Sinn Féin club held its inaugural meeting in August 1917 and, within months, meetings and rallies were being organized to heighten the movement's profile.[13] Brian Lacy has argued that the 'nationalists and the anti-partitionists were still stronger [than Sinn Féin] in Derry' when it came to overall political support in these years.[14] While it can be argued that this was fairly true, it fails to appreciate a more complicated picture that was showing strong embryonic signs of development.

As early as July 1916, Bishop McHugh was moving away from the IPP (due to Redmond's acceptance of partition) and had tried, unsuccessfully, to establish a new organisation called the Anti-Partitionist League. Under McHugh's leadership and the direction of his clergy, branches of the League were established in Derry, Omagh and Inishowen; but by autumn it had more or less collapsed as (nationally) home rule and the prosecution of the war eclipsed McHugh's concerns on partition. Throughout 1917, support for Sinn Féin grew, and many priests associated themselves with the movement in the belief that it was the organization able to prosecute a new anti-partition campaign. Indeed, the Revd James McGlinchey, dean of studies of St Columb's College (known affectionately as 'Dean' McGlinchey), actively canvassed support for Sinn Féin.[15] McGlinchey seems to have been to the forefront throughout 1917 in advancing the Sinn Féin cause, but although the bishop refrained from taking such a prominent Sinn Féin stance, no evidence has been found that he took McGlinchey to task.

In January 1918, Padraig Pearse's widow and daughter visited and were received by the Sinn Féin Club in Richmond Street. Both women lunched with the superioress of the Mercy Order, Pump Street, before attending a large meeting held in their honour, where 'the whole assemblage greeted the visitors with vociferous cheering when they entered'.[16] The *Journal* commented:

> Personally she felt the proudest mother in Ireland, and though her sacrifice might be termed great in having lost two sons, she was sure there were hundreds, nay thousands of Irish mothers capable of offering similar gifts on the altar of Irish unity.[17]

This visit was closely followed in February by the appearance of Eamon de Valera in St Columb's Hall ('the building being filled to overflowing'), where the audience included the Revd McGlinchey, the Revd James O'Doherty, Robert Whiteside, William Deane and J.B. Flanagan.[18] All these people were prominent locally, and again the input of the clergy should be noted. Although Desmond Murphy interpreted the clergy's influence as diminishing in the years immediately before 1920, it cannot be dismissed so lightly. Bishop McHugh remained silent after the onset of partition and the demise of the IPP, yet the appearance of clergymen at these meetings could not have happened without McHugh's approval.[19] The following months saw more meetings due to the conscription crisis, which solidified moderate nationalist support in the city solidly behind Sinn Féin. In an editorial under the heading 'The Conscription Cloud', the *Journal* said:

> When people talk about the appalling physical difficulty of chasing Irish conscriptionists over the hills and bogs, they are simply finding excuses for avoiding an unpleasant task … If the Unionist farmers' sons are yearning so deeply to be pressed into the army ranks, how is it that not a single one of the Ulster Unionist MPs accepted the repeated challenge of the *Ulster Guardian* to advocate the application of conscription from a public platform in his own constituency?[20]

Like the rest of Ireland, the arrival of the conscription issue in Derry went a long way to harnessing support for Sinn Féin, even at the expense of the Ancient Order of Hibernians. When the result of the East Cavan by-election was announced in June 1918, the *Journal* commented that it was

> A ringing declaration of the people's disgust and indignation at the shameful trickery of the British Government over the home rule issue, and … is the renewal of a firm and inflexible protest against the tyrannical resolve of those who would arbitrarily impose the crushing burden of conscription upon the shoulders of the country.[21]

After sons and loved ones failed to return from the killing fields of France and Belgium, the very reasons that drove people against those involved in the 1916 Easter Rising had now evaporated, to be replaced by a different ideology in 1918.[22]

The Westminster election of December 1918 – which became known as the Sinn Féin election – cast a long shadow over Irish politics as the new year approached. In Ulster, to maximize the catholic vote and reduce the number of instances that a Nationalist candidate would oppose a Sinn Féin candidate, the clergy under Cardinal Logue persuaded the two organizations to agree to an electoral pact.[23] To the clergy, and nationalism in general, the idea that two pro-nationalist candidates would contest a seat, split the vote and allow a unionist to win, was unthinkable. Therefore, Sinn Féin would contest four seats, as would the IPP. Derry was designated a Sinn Féin seat with the historian, Eoin MacNeill, standing on the pre-agreed ticket. The *Journal* called on Northern nationalists 'to uphold the flag of progress and liberty in every seat in Ulster by right of their voting strength that now belongs to them'; but there were dissenting voices: a letter published under the name 'Finn Valley' encouraged people to vote for the IPP and not Sinn Féin.[24] There is evidence that, had it not been for the active role played by the clergy, dissension between Nationalist and Sinn Féin supporters could have resulted in the loss of several seats in Ulster.[25] Both McHugh and Sinn Féin agreed that an accommodation was necessary if seats were not to be lost. Indeed, in a conciliatory letter published on 27 November, a Sinn Féin spokesperson was vociferous in his support of the bishop's stance. It also became apparent that McHugh donated £10 to MacNeill's campaign expenses, something at odds perhaps with the general belief that he was not overtly pro-Sinn Féin.[26] A large gathering of nationalists and Sinn Féin supporters occurred on 11 December in St Columb's Hall, where many clergy and businessmen again showed that the political drive originated from their quarters. Fr James McShane, Sinn Féiner and parish priest (and later dean of St Columb's), said they 'were determined that not even a sod of Ulster would be cut from Ireland, and by returning MacNeill, they would express that determination.'[27] MacNeill was returned triumphantly. The *Journal*, under the heading 'Exit the Elections: what next?' stated: 'Derry City, as we anticipated, was true to its splendid reputation to the National cause, and with most commendable spirit personal political predictions were sunk by many so as to hold the seat for an indivisible Ireland.'[28] The *Journal* said MacNeill had 'not come to Derry to make significant promises; he simply asked them to stand with him and the rest of the men who were making this fight for the rights of Ireland, on which depended the prosperity of the nation'.[29] This latter comment would have repercussions later, as 1919–20 would bring a fight for control of local government that would in turn ultimately bring Derry into conflict with MacNeill and Dáil Éireann in Dublin.

One final factor in MacNeill's success was the expansion of the franchise as a result of the Representation of the People Act. Derry's electoral roll, which had been important in previous elections (one notable election agent, Michael McDaid, was renowned for the attention he paid to the electoral franchise and for ascertaining who was and was not registered), took on even greater significance as the electoral roll increased from 6,000 to 16,000. One ingredient was the enfranchisement of women for the first time. Since many women lived and worked in the city, their vote was utilized to benefit MacNeill. Fr L. Hegarty, who chaired MacNeill's victory meeting in St Columb's Hall, mentioned this specifically and said the victory could not have been obtained without the female vote.[30] This success, taken in tandem with the electoral changes which had benefited nationalism, and coupled with the success of Sinn Féin nationally, gave local nationalists hope for the forthcoming political campaign as well as setting the scene for the local elections due to be held in 1920.

2. The local election, 1920

Although Derry remained relatively quiet throughout 1919, several incidents occurred that did not augur well for the new decade. Sir Robert Anderson, local unionist businessman, was elected mayor of the city for the fifth year in succession. Indeed, there was no sign of conciliation among unionists and Sinn Féiners in Derry, with the *Journal* commenting on the corporation: 'The political and sectarian discrimination against Nationalist members has never been departed from and it still holds the field.'[1] Nationally, Sinn Féin had taken 73 seats in December's election, decimating the IPP. True to their election manifesto, Sinn Féin declared they would not take their seats in Westminster, but worked immediately to establish a government in Dublin called Dáil Éireann. This situation rattled unionism, and, like the early months of 1914, the prospect of conflict rose considerably.

In July, Edward Carson (Ulster unionism's leader and one of the chief architects of partition) spoke of the possibility of violence and even civil war if the North was forced into a united Ireland, and, in Derry, there were several sectarian-related incidents, mainly surrounding the 12th of July celebrations. The *Journal* had this to say about celebrations throughout the North:

> This year the Twelfth was ushered in with a disgraceful orgy of rowdyism, reminiscent of the years immediately preceding the war, when insults were hurled at the majority of the citizens and a saturnalia of riot and revolver firing prevailed.[2]

In Derry, it was noted that the majority of the catholic inhabitants held aloft from the celebrations and left the field free to 'loyalists'. With the exception of 'rowdyism and revolver fire', the *Journal* stated that the Twelfth celebrations were 'an exceedingly tame affair' in the city. Interestingly, it also noted that some nationalist ex-soldiers erected an arch in the Bogside to the memory of the heroic dead of the Irish Brigade.[3] On 12 August, the Apprentice Boys of Derry's parade to celebrate the closing of the city's gates in 1688 was held. The *Journal* noted that 'as compared with pre-war years, a great improvement was observable in the demeanour of the processionists and sympathisers'. Referring to the absence of trouble-makers from 'Belfast, Lurgan, Portadown and other notorious Orange centres', it wryly remarked that the 'Belfast' accent could be heard occasionally, which in turn recalled 'the frightful days when it made the air reek in the use of abominable obscenities'.[4] It did refer, however, to windows being broken in houses occupied by catholics in the predominantly protestant Waterside, and acknowledged there was tension in the city.

Things took a turn for the worst when 5,000 members of the Ancient Order of Hibernians marched in Derry on 15 August. The AOH procession had been described in the *Journal* as 'a splendid display of the catholic manhood of Derry',[5] but rioting occurred on Ferryquay Street and Butcher Street. Although the Journal accused unionist leaders of being responsible for the trouble (citing the Revd King in Limavady for his inflammatory speeches) the paper also condemned the Hibernians for their behaviour too. It remarked that 'though the procession was of huge dimensions, still it was suspected that it would have been much larger'. The *Journal* criticized the 'deliberate object of discrediting the catholic and Nationalist people of the city' on the part of unionists as being the main reason for the trouble.[6] The march had been the first major street gathering of nationalism since MacNeill won the Derry seat in December 1918, and its message was clear: the cry from nationalist quarters was to have Derry included in the newly declared Irish state and not in a partitioned Ulster. In a letter subsequently published in the *Journal* on 1 September, Thomas Doran (Secretary, Demonstration Committee, AOH) categorically denied that soldiers were spat upon, and claimed that the major commanding the Dorset regiment had asked him to 'thank the people for their act of kindness (for serving tea)'.

In response to the initial success of Sinn Féin at the polls in December 1919, the British government introduced proportional representation as a means by which southern protestant unionism might dent future Sinn Féin electoral success. The first such opportunity would occur with the local government elections of January 1920. Here, the British administration believed that by abolishing the traditional 'first past the post' system, unionism in the cities and counties where Sinn Féin held power (but where they themselves formed a substantial minority of the population) would challenge and perhaps obstruct Sinn Féin aspirations. A booklet printed and published in 1919 by the government explained the strategy: 'the object of proportional representation is to give representation to parties in proportion to their electoral strength, and to secure the adequate representation of minorities.'[7]

In Derry, the letter and spirit of this legislation was carried through completely. As the city had a majority nationalist population, it followed that a nationalist majority in local government should be elected and that the unionist minority would have representation according to their own numbers. In its 18 August issue, the *Journal* published a short note stating that unless some gerrymandering accompanied the recent Proportional Representation Act, 'catholics will have a majority in the corporation'. The United Irish League, under the auspices of Charles O'Neill, DL, John Tracy, solicitor, and Michael McDaid, encouraged people to register their vote, as did the Sinn Féin electoral officers in the city (James Gallagher and Patrick Shiels).[8]

Unionists were aware of the electoral threat. The corporation proposed a motion whereby there would be 21 members for 19,958 voters against 19 members for 20,882; it was carried by 15 votes to 11. However, the *Journal* hoped that the Local Government Board would nullify this resolution in early October.

In September, the British government responded against this developing political landscape. Dáil Éireann was suspended, while in Derry extensive house raids were carried out by British troops. In St Columb's Hall, a meeting was held to protest against the 'scandalous attempt of the Unionist majority of the corporation to perpetuate an intolerable ascendancy control in municipal elections'. Joseph O'Doherty, Sinn Féin MP for Donegal, said: 'if every man and woman in Derry was now prepared to take the responsibility of citizenship they would win through in this crisis'. Councillor H.C. O'Doherty, local solicitor and a future mayor, said that 'it was with a view to strengthening the position of the Unionists of Ireland that the Proportional Representation Act was passed – not with the object of bettering the condition of the majority of the electors of Derry'.[9]

The Corporation employed William Walker, a Unionist agent, to deal with claims and objections to the PR motion passed earlier. His remit was to ensure that the re-drawing of electoral wards in the previous month would not spell an end to Unionist hegemony. The *Journal's* editorial of 22 October said that 'the duty of the Local Government Board is to act without prejudice or leanings to party in conformity with the legal requirements of the case' when speaking about nationalist Derry opposing the recent corporation motion. However, it was to no avail. On 10 November, the *Journal* reported that the Board had sanctioned the gerrymander:

> The action of the Derry corporation – the Unionist majority representing a minority of the citizens – was grossly unjust, but perfectly honest and straight from the Unionist point of view; the action of the Local Government Board in approving of this outrageous proposal is equally unjust, but in addition, it is thoroughly dishonest.

Immediately, nationalists challenged the board's decision by taking legal action in Dublin. This too was unsuccessful, and they were left hoping that the operation of the original proportional representation legislation would ultimately override the corporation's gerrymander.

But, if elected, what could a nationalist corporation achieve? Although Eoin MacNeill and several writers in the *Journal* believed that a victory was more than a possibility, national events were conspiring to reduce the impact that such a victory might have. By the middle of December 1919, Lloyd George had announced his Government of Ireland legislation that would eventually – 'officially' – partition the country, while the national leadership in Dublin seemed more preoccupied with financing the new administration and preparing for war against London. Against this background, MacNeill pronounced that 'despite the forces of ascendancy arrayed against them – whether in Dublin Castle, the King's Bench or the Revision Court – there is the possibility of Derry catholics gaining a victory'.[10] Joseph Devlin, nationalist leader in Belfast and confidant of the IPP leadership in Dublin, prophesied that partition was inevitable and that there would be dire consequences for Ulster catholics. The subsequent introduction of the Government of Ireland bill before parliament on 22 December made nationalists even more determined to show through the ballot box, at local government level, that the bill was a travesty and would be unworkable.[11] Both sides were confident. Unionism, through a series of gerrymandering tactics throughout the late 19th century and early 20th century had managed to control the city. (It had been remarked that the last nationalist mayor was one of the O'Neills in the 1690s.) The nationalist coalition was determined to break their hold.

In St Columb's Hall, Fr Lawrence Hegarty, curate at St Eugene's cathedral, presided over a raucous gathering of Sinn Féiners and nationalists. He spoke of how 'generations of Derrymen had laboured and made sacrifices',[12] while Hugh C. O'Doherty, councillor and respected solicitor, identified the 'two great issues' at hand – partition and the control of education. Local unionist representatives knew they were in danger of losing control of the corporation. The *Londonderry Sentinel* said 'any abstentions at the poll or errors … may place a Roman catholic mayor and Sinn Féin corporation in office in Derry' and, in a letter distributed to unionist supporters on the eve of the election, the Londonderry Unionist Association stated that 'to leave any one Unionist candidate out would be fatal'.[13] In reply, the *Journal* called: 'Catholics and Nationalists of Derry, rally to the popular cause to-morrow and answer this insult to your faith!'[14]

Both sides could not have asked for a better day to rally their respective troops. The *Journal* remarked on the fine weather on 14 January 1920 as well as the ready availability of transport in Derry city, as the use of the motorcar had become widespread.[15] First indications on polling day showed that there had been a high turnout. Both camps were delighted to see such a mix of young, old, male and female.[16] Although there were early cases of people spoiling their papers and of others making genuine mistakes, polling officers noted that 'as a rule a little soothing influence was brought to bear on the angry one and he completed his task satisfactorily'.[17]

The victory went to the nationalists, much to the consternation of Sir James Craig and the Unionist party in Belfast. By a majority of 21 seats to 19, they now held power on the corporation. Under the banner headline 'A Stiff Fight and a Great Victory', the *Journal's* editorial said:

> The Derry election results give the crowning touch to the outstanding fact that the tide of feelings now flows so strongly in the people's favour

> as to be no longer stayed in its course by the mildewed ramparts of reaction … The strong, sustained and unyielding determination of Derry Unionism to maintain its dominancy has been strikingly shown in this municipal election.[18]

The local unionist paper, the *Londonderry Sentinel*, did not share these views: 'We regard it as very deplorable by the adverse result in the South-East Ward control of civic affairs in Londonderry passes for the next three years into the majority of Sinn Féin Nationalist Corporators.'[19] Despite a heavy presence of soldiers from the Dorset regiment, who were deployed in the Carlisle Road area at potential flashpoints, and though rain fell heavily during the night, 'nationalist bands, followed by a huge crowd, paraded some of the streets, and there was great rejoicing, bonfires blazing in many streets.'[20] Although jubilation was in evidence, there were constraining voices. Fr Walter O'Neill, a catholic priest in the city, said it was 'the privilege of victors to show forbearance and generosity in their hour of triumph and he was sure that he was expressing their sentiments when he said that now that they had won they would show the toleration of the victor.'[21]

The Derry correspondent of the *Morning Post* wrote that 'Sinn Féin will be ruthless in its manipulation of corporation employment and Unionist workers will be misplaced.' The paper lamented the growth of the Roman catholic population in the city and laid the blame with the expansion of the shipbuilding industry. The *Irish News* congratulated 'Derry's steadfast Nationalists today on one of the most remarkable and important of the victories won by the forces of progress in Ulster'.[22]

The corporation met on Friday 30 January 1920 to elect the various committees and the mayor. By prior arrangement, Alderman Hugh C. O'Doherty was the agreed nationalist candidate and, as soon as he was elected, there 'was a scene of wild enthusiasm among the crowd which thronged the Chamber. Cheering continued for a couple of minutes, and broke into a lusty rendering of "God Save Ireland" and "The Soldier's Song". The Green flag, the Tricolour and Stars and Stripes were waved.'[23] However, in his inaugural speech, if he was intending to hold out an olive branch to unionism, O'Doherty's message was confusing. Initially, he thanked the Unionists for not proposing an opponent: 'It would not have served any useful purpose, but there is a certain amount of graciousness in the fact that they did not, for which I thank them', but he continued by recalling the days of unionist hegemony and criticized Sir Robert Anderson for overseeing it for so long.[24] He said:

> I do not wholly blame the Unionist members for the state of affairs that existed. They inherited an evil past and considered themselves bound to its tradition … To-day Derry comes into line with the rest of Ireland and its determination to compel the English Government to keep faith

> with Ireland and the world when she declared that she fought the last war for the liberty of small nations and their right to determine their own destiny.[25]

He then spoke about the issues that would occupy him over the coming years – water, housing and electricity, as well as the financial position at the corporation: 'it is my intention to have the finances of the city investigated … and give a true account of the state of the city's finances.'[26] Councillor Sir John McFarland agreed with the mayor that all should work together – Whig, Tory, Unionist and Nationalist – for the betterment of the city, and Councillor Elliott seconded the motion.[27] For the first time in its history, nationalism held control of local government in Derry. The mayor concluded in dramatic circumstances: 'Ireland's right to determine her own destiny will come about whether the Protestants of Ulster like it or not.'

3. The fight for independence

With the exception of August 1919, the last major violence in Derry had occurred in 1913 when the annual Orange parade on 12 August was the scene of serious rioting. From 1913 to 1919, the years passed relatively peacefully with only minor incidents reported. Interestingly, in late 1916 there were 5,559 Ulster Volunteers in Derry city and county as opposed to 4,446 National Volunteers (the Irish Volunteers numbered only 188).[1] Rifles available to each group tell their own story: nationalists possessed no more than 1,000 rifles on the eve of the corporation's victory in January 1920, whereas the UVF possessed almost one weapon per man. This was reinforced as early as 1913 when an RIC report noted: 'nearly all the Unionists of every age in Londonderry carry revolvers'.[2]

Within one week of Hugh C. O'Doherty being elected mayor, the army and RIC officers carried out extensive raids in the city over 5 and 6 February. The *Journal* reported 'that a quantity of ammunition, revolvers, hand grenades and seditious literature, military documents, etc., were seized'.[3] Although it does not specify from which side they came, it can be assumed (due to the reference to seditious literature) that most of these raids were carried out on nationalist/Sinn Féin homes. This was quickly followed by reports that several Derry Sinn Féin members – who had been arrested during the roundup – had been moved from the city to Mountjoy gaol in Dublin.[4] Nationalist Volunteers lost no time bringing disruption to local affairs. On two occasions in February, telegraph and telephone wires were cut in the Termonbacca area.[5] Tension grew throughout February and early March causing Bishop McHugh to cancel the St Patrick's Day parade for fear of violence; he called on nationalist Ireland 'to control her own destiny, to make her own laws, to utilise her own resources and in general to shape her own fortune without inflicting injury on any man or nation'. The modest conciliatory tone of such a statement was perhaps lost on the 'armed' unionist population of the city when he concluded: 'From first to the last the bill [Government of Ireland Act] is an insult to Nationalist and catholic Ireland.'[6]

Derry greeted the news of Tomás Mac Curtain's killing in March 1920 in Cork with horror.[7] He had recently been elected mayor of Cork and the parallel for Derry's own mayor was not lost on the city's nationalist population. It was also reported that the mayor of Wexford had received a death threat.[8] In the same week, British soldiers in Dublin shot several civilians near Portobello barracks, and it was reported that Derry gaol was now to be officially used as an internment camp; the *Journal* alleged that over 80 men were already being held in the prison, including MPs Joseph Sweeney and P.J. Ward;[9] even more prisoners were brought from Dublin, and the mayor was refused permission to visit Derry gaol to see conditions for himself. House raids continued (one prominent local nationalist activist, Hugh McGuinness, was raided on 3 April) and tensions continued to grow. Throughout April, rumours circulated that another rising was imminent. Reports show that the military had now replaced the police on beat duty, while the police themselves were carrying both revolvers and rifles for the first time. Ships were also searched when docking and material seized.[10] Several events conspired to precipitate rioting on the weekend of 17–18 April. It was reported that Patrick Shiels was now on hunger strike in Mountjoy gaol and in a serious condition. Attacks on police barracks nationally by the Irish Volunteers were reported, while the Irish Trades Council called for a strike as part of the national campaign being orchestrated from Dublin.[11] Skirmishes between nationalists and unionists broke out on Wednesday 14 April at the Great Northern Railway station; co-incidentally, soldiers removing a prisoner from the train to the gaol became the focal point for the agitation, which spilled over to the junction of Fountain Street and Long Tower Street, a scene that was to be repeated over the coming months. By Saturday 17 April, as the country descended into warfare, fierce rioting erupted in Derry after soldiers were attacked in various parts of the city. In retaliation, unionists and soldiers of the Dorset regiment engaged crowds of nationalists: 'during the night it was reported that gangs of unionists, sallying forth from Wapping Lane, Hawkin Street, and Fountain Street, had attacked and beaten catholics returning home'.[12] The Dorset regiment was confined to barracks for the next few days, and only ventured to the city side from Ebrington barracks (which was situated in the Waterside) when an army private, who had been killed accidentally, was buried in the city cemetery on 26 April.

By the end of April there were reports of police barracks in Co. Londonderry being attacked (one such attack was in Feeney) and news came that Patrick Shiels had been released and was returning to Derry along with several other prisoners.[13] Industrial unrest added to an already volatile situation. Railway clerks had approved strike action, while a bakery strike commenced on 4 May. House raids continued, this time in the Lecky Road area, and the first report of policemen being shot occurred under the *Journal* headline 'sensational affair in Derry'. Two RIC constables, Peter Henley and Richard McLaughlin, escaped serious injury when they were shot in separate locations over the weekend of 1–2 May. Within one week, another two police officers were injured when they were shot in Bishop Street. As the countryside descended into war and Westminster debated on the deteriorating situation, both communities in Derry were coming to terms with the partitioning of the country when Lloyd George published a new bill in London. The *Journal* said the bill 'would provide a single parliament for all

2 Hugh C. O'Doherty, mayor of Derry (*Photograph: O'Doherty family*)

Ireland, with the temporary exclusion of Ulster on the basis of a county option'.[14]

As the bread strike continued and the city slowly fell into chaos, the Irish Volunteers stepped up their campaign. Once again, Derry woke up on 14 May to read of attacks nationwide on police barracks, including Burnfoot, Co. Donegal, which was only a couple of kilometres from the city centre. In the city itself, masked men raided the tax office on Bishop Street, tying up staff and taking official papers.[15] Local unionism was infuriated when the corporation's meeting proposed that Lord French, a staunch supporter of Ulster unionism, be removed from the roll of freemen of the city. The *Journal* noted that 'it was reported that French was made a Freeman in August 1918 when his speeches were made noteworthy by the repetition of the words "No Surrender".'[16] The city was a powder keg. Irish Volunteers were active, and social unrest was extensive. Protestants were organizing themselves for an attack on the city by Irish Volunteers, who they believed would come from Donegal. Rumour and counter-rumour abounded, nationalists believing they were about to be delivered into an Irish Republic and unionists wondering what the future would hold in the light of recent overtures from Westminster. Street fighting and shooting had never before been so intensive or widespread. Both the *Journal* and *Sentinel* remarked on the extensive use of revolvers.

On Saturday 15 May 1920, Irish Volunteers in Lower Bridge Street shot the first policeman killed in Ulster. Sergeant Denis Moroney, a native of Clare, had been on duty when rival gangs fought at flashpoints between nationalist and unionist streets.[17] Rioting continued over the weekend and it was not long before the first catholic met the same fate. Bernard O'Doherty, an ex-soldier from Ann Street, was killed when he was hit by a sniper's bullet on Orchard Street. The *Journa*l reported for the first time that some of the rioters were carrying rifles.[18] Although both sides were eager to display their fervour for their own causes, the *Journal* laid the blame for the current outbreak at the door of Unionism, and acknowledged, prophetically, that the city's problems did not always rate highly on Dublin's agenda:

> The latest disturbances in Derry which have had calamitous results appear to have been deliberately provoked by an outburst of Orange rowdyism in Bridge Street ... This inherency of Orange aggressiveness and intolerance is a matter for the gravest apprehension in centres like Derry. It is a menacing factor by which localities South of the Boyne are never disturbed.[19]

Nationalists who were arrested on firearms charges proceeded not to recognize the courts. James Cullen, Lecky Road, when appearing before the assizes, stated that although he had no objection to the constitution of the court, 'as a soldier of the Irish Republic I do not recognize its authority'. As the *Journal* reported on the inquest held into the death of Bernard O'Doherty, it also carried the hearings from the house of commons relating to partition. The debate on whether six counties or nine should be excluded, a scenario that brought fear to both communities for very different reasons, was the talking point in the city. Several letter writers to the nationalist newspaper warned the city's citizens not to be sucked into the sectarian war that could come about if a political vacuum was created. One writer from Beragh, Co. Tyrone, who signed himself 'One who knows', said: 'The nationalists of Derry and other areas are great fools if they are drawn into a riot for the purpose of getting shot or bayoneted by military or police; evidently that is the object now in view.'[20] Although violence in Derry was extensive, the death toll had not come anywhere near that of other counties in Ireland, notably Dublin, Tipperary, Cork and Longford.

Still, the violence in Ulster would turn much worse in the coming months, and rather than describing it as 'sudden' (as Phoenix has argued), evidence exists to show that it was premeditated.[21] Dáil Éireann was aware of the deteriorating situation in Ulster for it received correspondence from the Belfast-based publisher, Forbes Patterson, called 'Report on political situation in north east Ulster'.[22] In it, Patterson encouraged Dublin to establish a newspaper in the North to fight British propaganda and to encourage a workers' revolt against British rule. The general secretary of Dáil Éireann, Diarmuid Ó hEigceartuigh, took a less than flattering view on Patterson's report and idea for a newspaper: 'There are a few interesting views expressed in it, although the efficacy of a propagandist paper for military purposes may be questionable.'[23] More importantly, in light of what was to happen in June, July and August, Patterson stated:

> Signs have appeared in the last month [April 1920] of business men being trained as spotters and Orangemen being organised into vendetta against nationalists … home rule for the six North East countries is in my opinion a setting of the stage for a pogrom against catholics. The object of the British would seem to be towards enticing the Irish Volunteers into the open by producing a state of mob war in the North East, and thus crushing the whole national movement.

He continued: 'Unionism is still the strongest political force in Ulster but it is being steadily broken up by labour. Hibernianism is still strong but also weakening. Republicanism is weak and, comparatively speaking, is not advancing, while Liberalism is now a tangible quantity.' He believed that Labour would inevitably become pro-English if left to its own devices, despite the influence of Councillor James Baird (a protestant member of Belfast corporation) who was moving towards an Irish national position. He continued:

> Any paper placed in the hands of Labour in Ulster would gravitate to the strongest section, which is based on English traditions of Labour, and that our policy ought to be, to run such a paper ourselves with a view towards binding to us and strengthening the hands of those Labour men of Irish sympathies.

Given that the Democratic Programme, a radical social agenda to bring justice and equality to the nation's citizens that was part of the First Dáil's social reform in 1919, had gone by the wayside as a result of the political war being fought, it is not surprising that Dublin was lukewarm to Patterson's proposals. Indeed, among the many men involved in processing the current war of independence were many Roman catholic nationalists who had little time for socialism and were content to use Labour and the trade union movement for their own political purposes.[24]

Throughout April and May, the British army kept a high profile as both sides in Derry issued death threats, with partisan notices being nailed to lamp-posts and houses being daubed with graffiti. The *Journal* played down death threats to unionists and said that pranksters issued them with no validity: 'Derry has a liberal quota of practical jokers, who are ever ready for a prank, no matter how grim.'[25] House raids continued while nationally the country was hit by a railway strike.[26] One local man, James Wray, was shot and wounded in Bridge Street, and catholic families in Wapping Lane were forced to flee after threats by local unionists. At the corporation meeting on Friday 29 May, the earlier motion to have Lord French removed from the roll of freemen was approved. Unionist aldermen and councillors were enraged, as was the general unionist population in the city.[27]

By June 1920, violence was fierce, premeditated, and far from sudden.[28] Indeed, it is debatable whether or not it could simply be labelled as sectarian. The month began with the burning of two RIC barracks in Co. Londonderry (Park and Ballyronan) while there were daily reports of masked men roaming streets bordering catholic and protestant housing. On Sunday 6 June, shots were fired in John Street, and within two weeks there were several more incidents of indiscriminate revolver fire. After an attack on catholics in the Prehen area of the Waterside on 16 June, the *Journal* accused certain sections of the unionist population of wanton involvement in such incidents over the previous weeks: 'without interference on the part of the police, have night after night since the middle of May kept up a reign of terror in that part of the city, where apparently they are to have a free hand to carry on their murderous escapades.'[29]

The presiding judge at the assizes, Judge Osbourne, was not amused by the lack of police intervention 'when Fountain Street is ready to take a hand along with the police'. This admission that the police were standing idly by and not protecting the citizens was reinforced by a court case in July.[30] This suggests that there was collusion in Derry between the military authorities, the RIC, and unionist squads based on the Ulster Volunteer Force (UVF). One writer of the period (a secretary in the publicity department of the Dáil) alleged that there was a force called the 'Civilian Guards' operating in Derry under the auspices of Dublin Castle.[31] In a letter to the *Journal*, signed 'Ratepayer', another writer maintained he had 'observed Unionists coming across the Bridge acting in a most provocative and blackguardly manner, with two policemen silently looking on.' Collusion and apathy on the part of the authorities was about to prove fatal indeed.

As a result of the Prehen incident, notices were nailed to trees stating that 'any Sinn Féiner found in Prehen or Prehen Wood after this date will be shot on sight, signed 14 June 1920'. In an article which appeared in the *Journal* many years later, it was alleged that a protestant gentleman sent word to Dublin that the Dorset regiment had given weapons and ammunition to unionists.[32] However, to date, no evidence has surfaced to confirm this.

On Saturday 20 June, a scuffle developed at Bishop Street between rival factions before unionists unleashed a fusillade of shots down Albert Street and Fountain Street into Bishop Street and Long Tower Street. One man, John O'Neill, was injured; but another, John McVeigh, was killed. John Farren died shortly afterwards having been hit by a ricochet bullet. Another group of Orangemen came over from London Street before travelling down Bishop

Street, where Edward Price was shot at the entrance of the Diamond Hotel. Liam Brady, a member of Fianna Éireann in Derry at the time, alleged that 'an ex-army sergeant' led this group.[33] Taking up positions in Butcher Street, they fired shots down Fahan Street, killing another man (Thomas McLaughlin) and injuring a woman who went to his aid. Also to die that night at the hands of unionist gunmen was James Doherty. Brady believed a drunken squabble had been the spark for the violence (an explanation some espoused in the *Londonderry Standard*).[34] The *Journal* editorial of the same day stated: 'That most desirable condition latterly has been departed from because of the recrudescence of violence and unchecked "loyalist" terrorism.' Throughout Saturday night, street fighting occurred at many junctions where nationalist and unionist streets met, with unionist firepower overwhelming. By Sunday, the police and army had restored an uneasy calm to the flashpoints, but this did not stop the *Journal* on Monday accusing soldiers of standing idly by while unionist gunmen had a free hand. Indeed, Brady repeated this allegation: 'No police or soldiers came to protect the nationalists although there was a battalion of the Dorset regiment and hundreds of police in the city at the time.'[35] From the reporting in all the newspapers it is clear that those killed died as a result of firing from the city walls and Fountain area. Even the *Irish Independent* noted: 'It is undeniable that the police and military know the names of 50 or more Unionists who for some time past have kept up a reign of terror.'[36] In separate incidents, stores were looted and, in one instance, in William Street, a company of Irish Volunteers with hurley sticks was despatched to protect shops. Fire tenders were burned and groups of unionist and nationalist supporters exchanged shots in the Waterside, Carlisle Road, William Street and Bond Street.

As local newspapers disagreed on the origins of Saturday evening's attacks in their Monday editions, workers on their way to the docks came under sporadic fire from across the river and snipers soon appeared on rooftops in the city to command strategic junctions: 'snipers on Walker's monument, the protestant Cathedral, Bishop Street, the Orange Hall and the Masonic Hall in Magazine Street had a commanding view over most of the nationalist area and things were such that for a time the city was completely in the hands of the Orangemen'.[37] By Wednesday 23 June, another four men had died (William O'Kane, John Gallagher, Howard McKay and Joseph Plunkett), but the Irish Volunteers were now out in force. The *Journal* noted for the first time that Volunteers were carrying rifles and, on 25 June, they were referred to as the Irish Republican Army (IRA). By Wednesday, machine guns were also in use and unionists had been driven from many of their key positions. The *Journal* again remarked: 'the loss of Derry to the Unionist cause cannot be retrieved by the loss of so many Nationalist lives ... Nationalists cannot be expected to "lie down" under a raid any more than they would expect Unionists to do the same.'[38]

Life in the city stood still, and few, other than the combatants, ventured out. There were gun battles throughout the city, including in the grounds of St

Columb's College, which was the scene of much bitter fighting. Referring to the original attack on the Long Tower, the *Journal* reiterated that it was 'entirely premeditated and unprovoked'.[39] On Friday, extra troops arrived in the city and a Royal Navy destroyer laid anchor in the river Foyle. In the house of commons, MPs such as Lord Cecil and Major O'Neill accused Bonar Law of not supplying the city with enough troops once the violence started. By the end of June there were over 1,500 soldiers and 150 RIC men in Derry, although prior to the fighting it was alleged in the house of commons that only 250 soldiers were on duty.[40] Denis Henry, Irish attorney-general, in a Dáil Éireann debate on Derry on Tuesday 22 June, said the explanation for so much trouble was that 'it was an old city, full of rabbit-holes, from which men could shoot and retire at once out of sight. Derry differed from Dublin, where they shoot men in the back. In Derry there was an element of fight.'[41] With the arrival of troops, a stalemate developed. Liam Brady alleged that the IRA was planning a large-scale attack on Thursday 24 June when news came through that extra troops were being sent; he also accused the authorities of using the violence to gather intelligence on the strength of the IRA in the city. However, another IRA officer, Lieutenant M. Sherrin, although agreeing that this too was the reason for the abandonment of the attack, accused Republicans of cowardice when faced with the new contingent of British troops:

> Our force other than the IRA Company which occupied HQ could not be complimented on their conduct, after the first onslaught of the British they turned into a panicky mob. I was at the Headquarters at this time, and the terrible rush to the College; the discarding of rifles, ammunition etc., and hasty disappearance of the men was not edifying.[42]

But criticism of the government's stance came from many quarters. Inaction, it was alleged, had cost the lives of many people. The city magistrates had requested extra troops on Monday 21 June and, not receiving a reply by Wednesday, the following was then sent to the chief secretary:

> City magistrates assembled today are greatly alarmed by no action having been taken by the government in response to previous telegram. They consider situation desperate and growing worse hourly. The food supply is running out, and gas supply almost exhausted. More lives lost last night. Magistrates request reply and assurance from government of immediate action to allay panic amongst citizens.[43]

Catholic families were driven from their homes in Carlisle Road, Abercorn Road, Harding Street and other unionist-dominated areas in the city before martial law was declared on Saturday 26 June. The *Journal* reported that catholic homes continued to be raided whereas protestant homes remained unscathed:

> Raids have not so far been made on the houses of protestants though it is notorious that a catholic was shot dead by a sniper concealed on the premises of a prominent Unionist in the city … It is understood that catholic members of the local constabulary force tendered their resignations as a protest against the conduct of certain soldiers who it is alleged permitted looting to go on and who actually shared the loot with Unionists.[44]

Its editorial continued: 'The fires of sectarian passion in Derry have been set alight by a Unionist conspiracy in Belfast and London in order to maintain its squalid ascendancy in the North.' The accusation of collusion was immediate. On 28 June, the *Journal* called for an inquiry into the conduct of soldiers during the previous week's violence (Dorset regiment), and a witness to the killing of Thomas Farren stated that the deadly shots came from Fountain Street, where a cordon had been established by the Dorsets.[45] One of the most interesting incidents of the period occurred when British soldiers arrested several men, whom the *Journal* daubed the 'German Riflemen' (due to the Mauser rifles they carried), in the Waterside district on Wednesday 23 June. When released on bail, they said they were doing a service to the community by protecting the post office in Melrose Terrace.[46] When they appeared before petty sessions court on 1 July, it was apparent from evidence given that they were members of a UVF patrol. Lieutenant Wattley, who was in command of the soldiers, said he asked the men the password to which they replied, 'Scotland'. He had believed the password to be 'Ulster Volunteer Force' and with his evidence it became apparent to those in the court that there was some level of co-operation between unionist gunmen and the British army. However, it is not known how high this went in Derry's chain of command. Liam Brady alleged that communications between the Waterside and cityside conducted by 'expert Morse and semaphore signallers', indicating that the trouble was not the work 'of a number of irresponsible youths'.[47] Other evidence came from the inquest courts and the various charges that were brought before defendants. James Gray was charged with the murder of William O'Kane. But the inquest concluded: 'We find that William James O'Kane met his death on the 22nd June by a bullet fired from an automatic pistol.' The *Journal* asked why the verdict wasn't murder, whereas the *Sentinel* didn't even report it.[48] It seemed that key protestants who had the misfortune of finding themselves in front of the courts were to be treated leniently.[49] The final indictment on the whole episode of late June came from the mayor, Hugh C. O'Doherty:

> It was deplorable to think that in this twentieth century citizens' hands should be raised against citizens' lives. It was deplorable to think that for any cause men should band themselves together for the purpose of destroying a section of their fellow citizens … No adequate measures

> were taken (by British army). Bands of military were placed here and there. What did they do? On the first day they actually fraternised with the bands that were terrorising the city. They took no steps whatsoever to control them.[50]

In Dublin, Michael Hayes, referring to the unionist campaign in July 1920, which was to have included Belfast, Lisburn and Derry, said: 'the Derry business frizzled out badly. The catholic was too numerous and determined to make the attempt safe, and this outpost must await until the course of events gives better hope of success.'[51] In one respect, it was obvious that the provisional government believed Derry was being held, but there was little or no evidence to show that this could be done for an indefinite period of time.

By the beginning of July, Derry was burying 20 people, 15 of whom were catholics. One of those killed was Joseph McGlinchey (his father, James McGlinchey, was one of the most senior Irish Volunteer figures in the city at the time), and the funeral also took place of Howard McKay, son of Marshall McKay, leader of the Apprentice Boys of Derry. With the introduction of martial law, a curfew was imposed; Orange parades were banned. The *Journal* believed that, until such parades were without sectarianism, they should continue to be banned:

> Until better manners are learned and are put into practice there is only one sure skin-cure for this Orange rash. Presently the attending physician is Colonel Chaplin and his "prescription" is found within the four corners of the published proclamation.[52]

At the end of the month the IRA was in open conflict with British forces and issuing statements concerning the maintenance of peace in the city. On 25 June one statement decreed that public houses were to close between the hours of 9.00 p.m. and 10.00 a.m., a tacit admission that alcohol was playing some part in the whole affair. Indeed, other statements issued said they would defend catholic areas as well as St Columb's College, the grounds of which had seen some bitter fighting at the height of the violence.[53] There were many arrests arising out of curfew violations, most of whom were catholics, as well as numerous shootings.[54] In its 19 July editon, the *Journal* reported that over 8,000 people were without work in the shirt industry as a result of the ongoing strike and social unrest, and the same edition carried news of the death of Commissioner Gerald Smyth, which was to have implications for Ulster nationalists within days.[55] By 23 July, the first reports were coming through from Belfast of shootings and expulsions from the shipyards. The *Journal* reported: 'Belfast joins war on Irish catholics'. Interestingly, the *Journal* also published a letter from Forbes Patterson, who had been in contact with Dublin earlier:

> The sectarian bitterness which in their hey-day they raised no finger to allay, nay, which I have known them to deliberately fan, will pull about their ears the unholy temple which they have built. They stand without credit from God or man, and remember the Christ who whipped the money changers out of the House of God, I cannot feel.[56]

On 30 July, two people were shot in Sugarhouse Lane by the British army after it was alleged they had violated curfew hours, while it was noted that, with the arrival of the curfew, people began to obstruct military patrols. Glass was strewn across roads so vehicle tyres would burst, and before long soldiers were patrolling on foot.[57] What was noticeable was the sudden downturn in IRA activity. Although four companies were formed in late June (plus an engineering company under the command of Charles Mawhinney), military activity was far from the level exercised in June. By the beginning of September, headquarters in Dublin had upgraded Derry to divisional headquarters:

> We have no intention of tamely allowing a big concentration on the North-West any more than in the South-West … it becomes now imperative for our units in Donegal, Derry, and Tirone to develop their Organisation and Information service, to improve their training, and above all to study and re-study the ground.[58]

By September, the IRA command in Dublin believed that there had not been enough harassment of enemy troops. But the city was not totally without incident: the Lecky Road police barracks was burned on 5 August and the railway line between Crolly and Kinkasslagh, operated by the Londonderry and Lough Swilly Railway Company, was destroyed by IRA men.[59] Minor incidents occurred too: although the Relief of Derry parade was proscribed, it did not stop local unionists from raising a Union Jack at the head of Bridge Street, a staunchly nationalist area. Republican flags duly appeared, but a major confrontation was averted when British soldiers removed the Union Jack. On 16 August, the *Journal* reported that over 2,000 unionists marched around – before curfew – terrorizing residents in the Long Tower area; clearly, tensions continued to remain high. Again, throughout August, the local papers carried reports of the ongoing war in Belfast, and extensive coverage was also given on 23 July to the killing of Inspector Oswald Swanzy in Lisburn.[60] This precipitated one of the worst nights of violence in Ireland, when catholic homes and businesses were burned as a result of Swanzy's death and many catholics were expelled from the town.[61]

Isolated incidents of fighting continued in the city, and it was reported that unionists were still holding the bridge despite a heavy police and army presence. On 23 August, Robert John Mitchell, a unionist who had been found guilty of shooting into a house in Nailor's Row (near Bishop Street), was freed on bail indefinitely. Indeed, such incidents emphasized the duality of law in the city. In another court case, William Glass, the son of an RIC man, was charged with shooting (not attempted murder) Hugh Murray on 23 June. A soldier gave evidence saying shots were fired by a person who happened to be standing with other soldiers of the Dorset regiment; a witness, captain Walter H. Miles, said: 'The impression left on my mind was that it was from the group (behind soldiers). I started running and asked my men what was happening.' Asked if he could state positively that the two shots heard came from the civilians, Miles said that while he could not swear positively that civilians fired the two shots (because he did not examine their rifles), he had no reason to doubt that they were responsible. It is interesting to note that the captain's evidence corroborated that of the injured man. Later, two privates swore that Captain Miles was lying; but it is difficult to know if they were telling the truth, for one of them, Private J. Whatley, was not at his station when the shooting occurred: by saying he saw what had happened, he avoided admitting his dereliction of duty.[62]

At the end of August, disturbances in Belfast over a two-day period left 11 dead and many injured. The *Journal* reported that, in one street in the Shankill district of Belfast, a banner hung across the road saying, 'protestants, avenge young McKay, of Derry'.[63] As Derry watched from the sidelines, Belfast burned. Although Derry was historically more important to unionism, Belfast, where 170 buildings had now been destroyed since July, was the centre of power in the northern half of the country. The vast majority of IRA activity was concentrated in the greater Belfast area, as was the backlash from the RIC, army, and unionist death squads. There can be no doubt that a war was being fought, between two ideologies, two religions, and two forms of government. One republican and self-ruling, the other imperial, loyal to king and the British empire.

The IRA was also active in Donegal at the end of August, and in Derry unionists engaged in revolver firing in the Waterside on 2 September, while shots were fired at soldiers in William Street. By 8 September, extensive raiding was being carried out in the city, this time in the Cross Street, Glendermott Road and Dungiven Road areas. A local councillor, James McClean, was arrested in William Street for being in possession of seditious literature and was released on bail, although the charges were later dropped. The army raided the predominantly unionist Wapping Lane and Fountain Street, yet there was no reporting in the press of the reason. House raids continued throughout the month, but one incident did not go unnoticed. On 15 September, the *Journal* carried a small news piece relating to the establishment of a special constabulary for Ulster to assist the army and police in their campaign against the IRA. This too would have serious repercussions for stability over the coming months.

On 22 September, Mass was celebrated in the Long Tower church for the 'spiritual welfare' of Tomás Mac Curtain, the mayor of Cork who had been killed in January. Many schools and businesses closed as a mark of respect. Within days, the *Journal* wrote that 'uniformed men' had delivered letters to prominent Republicans containing the following typewritten notice:

> In some districts loyalists and members of his Majesty's forces have received notices threatening the destruction of their houses in certain eventualities. Under these circumstances it has been decided that for every loyalist house so destroyed the houses of a Republican leader will be similarly dealt with. It is naturally to be hoped that the necessity for such reprisals will not arise, and, therefore, this warning of the punishment which will follow the destruction of loyalists' houses is being widely circulated.[64]

Unionists in Carlisle Road shot Francis O'Hara on 28 September, while the Derry–Carndonagh train was cancelled as the crew refused to work due to the presence of two armed policemen on the train; a later train was cancelled for the same reason.[65] The crews were promptly suspended. October and November 1920 saw their fair share of violence in Derry, not all of it republican. House raids by the army continued unchecked, mainly conducted on nationalist and republican homes and offices, and the bridge remained under the control of armed unionists, much to the distress of nationalists who tried to cross it. Indeed, on many occasions, nationalists used boats to cross the river Foyle rather than confront unionists on the bridge. On 18 October, Constable John Flaherty was shot and killed near Mullan's Pub, Bishop Street, near the city walls. It was reported in both the *Sentinel* and *Journal* that, prior to the shooting, police arrested a unionist called Cameroon Finlay on Carlisle Road.[66] The *Journal* reported witnesses as saying that some of the soldiers shook hands with Finlay when he was being taken to the police station. Finlay had recently been court-martialled in connection with a shooting incident in the Waterside, but was found not guilty. The *Journal* alleged that Flaherty was shot as a result of Finlay's arrest. Flaherty, who was 46, was a catholic from Co. Galway.[67]

On 6 November 1920, IRA soldiers challenged two policemen at the Customs House to take their weapons.[68] The policemen refused to surrender and in the ensuing confrontation both were shot (Sergeant T. Wiseman and Constable George Waters). In reprisal, RIC men in mufti with their faces covered appeared after curfew and took revenge. In William Street, they fired into Charlie Breslin's shop before proceeding to John Doherty's shed next to Watts Distillery. The shed was torched. In the ensuing fire, 'residents in the locality could hear the agonising screams of the animals but no-one dare venture out'.[69] The police went to the home of Michael O'Doherty, father of Joseph, but the grenade that was thrown through the window failed to explode. They then destroyed the Doherty's butcher shop in Sackville Street and Patrick Hegarty's tobacconist store on Foyle Street. It is interesting to note that this attack was not random, but planned, with most premises selected belonging to IRA men, their families or supporters. Such attacks were commonplace in Belfast and other areas, but Derry city itself had been spared from such incidents. This particular November night changed that.

The evening's violence was complete when three policemen were found wounded in Foyle Street, one of whom, Constable Hugh Kearns from Monaghan, died later from his injuries. Brady alleged that, at the inquest, the fire brigade superintendent said the men were in civilian clothes and had opened fire on the tender. Additional evidence supports this view and reinforces that taken by Michael Farrell in *Northern Ireland: the Orange state* that the policemen formed part of a reprisal squad that was operating in the city.[70] The British army had mistaken them for IRA soldiers, as they were out of uniform and masked. Jim Herlihy states that Kearns was killed accidentally, and his service record shows he died from 'gunshot wounds on duty'.[71]

The *Journal* reported on 10 November from Kearns' inquest; in evidence, it was clear that the constable was shot by the military and may have been attempting to shoot at a fire tender. This, Head-Constable Cornelius O'Donoghue dismissed, as he did the claim that Kearns was one of several police officers in plain clothes. The affair did not end there. At a special sessions court for the hearing of compensation claims in February 1921, several of the policemen denied, under cross examination, that officers broke ranks from Victoria barracks and were partly responsible for the bloodshed. Asked why constables were in plain clothes when they were shot in Foyle Street, Head-Constable O'Donoghue took a different tack and said that it was normal for him to approve of this. This ran contrary to the evidence of Constable James Henaghan who said that he 'had never been out in plain clothes before'. O'Donoghue, incensed at this remark, said that that was his fault and that the officer (Henaghan) should not have said that.[72] Mr Babington KC produced one witness, James Trimble, superintendent of the fire tender, who stated under oath that they drove down to Foyle Street via the Diamond, Carlisle Road, and John Street before coming parallel to the Criterion Hotel, where they saw armed masked men with rifles. When asked if there was a volley of shots from Butter Market (as claimed by the officer in charge) he said No, and proceeded to allege that it was his impression that the first shot was fired by the men on the street (who subsequently transpired to be policemen). The hearing was then adjourned.

Although the recent analysis by Augusteijn states that the object of the attack was to acquire weapons (a view taken from Liam Brady's later testimony) this is at odds with other aspects of Brady's recollections which states that arms and ammunition were plentiful.[73] Another possible reason for the attack at this time was the arrival in the city, on 31 October, of Black and Tans, soldiers hired by the government to supplement the police force in Ireland and who had a fearsome reputation nationwide. Perhaps in Derry the IRA was marking the arrival of the new force, or they were trying to increase their activity as a result of requests from headquarters in Dublin to do so. On the first of the month, the local papers carried notice of the formal establishment of the Ulster Special Constabulary (USC).[74] There were three groupings – 'A' specials (full-time); 'B' specials (part-time); and 'C' specials, who were to be used for occasional duty, mainly in the districts where they lived. Ominously for the IRA campaign in Derry and the six counties under the threat of partition, the *Journal* stated that 'all classes will be armed similar to the regular forces, and will be under their own officers, but in the execution of duty will be subject to the control of the police authorities.'[75]

By the end of November, events outside Derry eclipsed those of the city itself. In London, the third reading of the Government of Ireland bill took place on 11 November, while all the local papers carried reports of the infamous Bloody Sunday killings in Dublin on Sunday 21 November. Derry republicans were shocked to learn of the deaths in Dublin of Richard McKee and Peter Clancy, and continued to grapple with industrial unrest.[76] Whereas in the rest of the country Labour had been successfully harnessed to fight the war against British rule, in Derry, as in other northern areas, it was a hindrance. In the six northern counties, the trade union movement put loyalty to religion and king before co-workers.[77] The shipyards had made 100 people redundant while a lockout continued at the local Watts Distillery.[78] The *Journal* reported that Eoin MacNeill had been arrested in Dublin while also noting that arms and ammunition had been landed in Derry to arm the USC.[79] Again there was extensive trouble in the city over the weekend of 27–28 November, with many windows being smashed in both catholic and protestant areas. The army continued their unrelenting campaign of house raids, and by the end of the year, St Columb's Hall, so long a nationalist meeting place in the city, had been commandeered by a detachment of the Yorkshire Light Infantry. While the Government of Ireland bill was confirmed and received the royal assent effectively leading to partition on 21 December, neither side was prepared to remember 25 December in a Christian spirit. The *Journal* reported on 29 December that Christmas Day was passed in the Carlisle Road area by rioting.

With the exception of isolated incidents (such as the cutting of communication lines), the IRA continued to be inactive in the early months of 1921, the one major exception being the successful jailbreak and rescue of Frank Carty who had been shot and captured by Black and Tans in Tubercurry, Co. Sligo.[80] The raiding party included Captain Charles McGuinness,[81] Dominick Doherty, and B. Doherty. Carty was taken from the city by sea on a boat called the *Carricklee*, which belonged to a Norwegian fisherman sympathetic to the republican cause.[82] However, most media reports refer to minor rioting, stone-throwing, and house raids, although shots were fired in the Midland Railway Station when armed men tried to board a train that had just arrived.[83] By the middle of the month, the first USC constabularies were active in the city, and by February local republicans seemed more preoccupied with enforcing the Belfast Boycott than using the weapons Liam Brady alleged the movement possessed. The boycott had been sanctioned in Dublin in September 1920 at the instigation of Sinn Féin members from Belfast, notably Denis McCullough and Sean MacEntee. Although most commentators saw it as a direct response to the plight of the catholic community in the city, one prominent clergyman, Bishop MacRory, primarily saw the boycott as a means of preventing partition.[84] In Derry, two IRA volunteers, Patrick Shiels and P. Fox, oversaw the campaign.[85] How well 'republican Derry' heeded the campaign can be gauged from two letters that appeared in the *Journal* on 11 and 23 February respectively:

> Derry readers should now carefully read the statement of the Star correspondent in to-day's *Independent* to the effect that a big trade offensive in the South and West is being organised by the Belfast merchants. The offensive is also being carried out in Derry. Belfast goods are being offered on exceptional low terms. Now is the time to be on the alert. If those people who have been shouting 'No partition' would stop their shouting and carry out the boycott Sir James Craig's little conventicle would never meet, signed 'Business'.

> There is a matter I would like to bring to the notice of the Derry Committee of above. The protestant shopkeepers of Derry, and especially in the Waterside district, are stocking nothing but Belfast goods, and what do we find? Their best customers nearly all catholics. The committee should try and devise some means of bringing home to these people – some of those pose as patriots – their duty in a matter so important to the 40,000 catholics who are starving at the hands of the pogromists of Belfast, the upholders of civil and religious liberty. Things are shaping in a way just now that Derry merchants and shopkeepers may find that unless the unforeseen happens they will be brought under the boycott, too. Unfortunately there is catholic shopkeepers still dealing in Belfast goods, as only yesterday I was in a catholic shop and saw Belfast commodities for sale. You will always find such types in every community.

Whether the same author penned both is debatable, but the general point was that nationalists in the city were not doing enough to isolate unionism. Augusteijn, writing of the violence in June 1920, touches upon this ambivalent attitude. In this instance, the IRA, like their counterparts in the UVF, co-operated to maintain order.[86] While the rest of the country descended into chaos, Derry volunteers were perhaps not as pro-active as they might have been for the republican cause.

There was serious rioting in March sparked by unionists marching around the Diamond area in military formation. One letter writer to the *Journal* said that 'as a witness of the incident, can you tell me why a unionist mobilisation of rowdies were allowed to assemble at Carlisle Square on Friday evening last and march in military formation to the Diamond, attack and beat catholics without any interference of the custodians of the peace?'[87] Perhaps as a direct result of this action, military pickets were positioned on the Diamond on 25 March, yet within one week, one of the most sustained nights of IRA attacks since June 1920 occurred. On 1 April, Sergeant John Higgins was shot dead at the junction of Windsor Terrace and Creggan Street, and a military post on Strand Road near the City Electrical Station was attacked with bombs and gunfire. In this latter incident three soldiers were injured. A short time later there was an attack on the RIC barracks at the junction of Nelson Street and Lecky Road: one RIC constable and a 'special' were injured. Later, a British soldier, Private J. Whyte, was shot dead when a weapon was accidentally discharged. Several civilians were also injured during the attacks.[88]

It is unusual, given the level of IRA activity throughout the country, that Derry's input to the war of independence should have been so sporadic. In many ways, the Derry Brigade was conspicuous by its absence. Augusteijn writes at length about dissension within the ranks of the organization as well as other factors contributing to the low level of IRA activity.[89] Seemingly, few members were willing to risk their lives for their country, perhaps not so surprising after the losses sustained in the war of 1914–18. Yet there is no doubt that local commanders such as Peadar O'Donnell, Patrick Shiels and Frank Carney disagreed on a strategy to execute the war in the city. Liam Brady talked about things they intended to do rather than events that actually happened. In one instance, he recalls how 'various districts were visited with the intention of making it tough for the British raiding parties, by blowing up bridges, by trenching and blocking the roads, and other types of instruction'.[90] In reality, local newspapers carried little evidence of such activity, while IRA raids were restricted by the presence of three battalions of British soldiers, plus the RIC, plus the newly arrived Ulster Special Constabulary and Black and Tans. One other factor was the tightly knit nature of the community: almost everyone knew each other. As one RIC county inspector remarked in February: 'The Derry city company of the IRA is no doubt ever watchful for an opportunity to strike a blow, but the Ulster Volunteers and the Orange lodges watch its members too carefully to permit of their doing much at present.'[91]

The advent of elections for the new Northern parliament in Belfast along with signs that both Irish and British representatives were active in coming to a compromise dented the military campaign. In a city where constitutional nationalism was as dominant as Sinn Féin's doctrine, notice in April of an election pact between Nationalists and Sinn Féin for the elections in May was not surprising.[92] April and May also saw several buildings burned, mainly in the Waterloo Street vicinity.[93] An end to military activity was more or less guaranteed with the announcement that de Valera had met Sir James Craig, leader of northern unionism and future prime minister of Northern Ireland. On 6 May the *Journal* said it was an important development:

> The meeting between the two leaders may be regarded as important, in view of Sir James Craig's statement in Banbridge on Monday, that he was prepared to meet Mr De Valera and his colleagues at any time he wished to do so, and Mr De Valera's statement in his proclamation, that in home affairs Sinn Féin stood for such devolution of administration and authority as would make for the satisfaction and contentment of all sections of the people.

The May election passed off without serious incident being reported and was followed by the announcement of the Truce on 11 July 1921.[94] Between July and Christmas of 1921, the city remained quiet with only isolated incidents reported. Even the August 'Relief' parade passed over without much comment:

> The most notable thing about it being the way it was shunned – save for a few extremists – by the great mass of the protestants and Presbyterian citizens. The better class people avoid a demonstration which only serves to keep alive a rancorous and un-Christian spirit of wrath and defiance ... they were celebrating the relief of Derry, and no greater relief could come to Derry than that as a result of all the present debating there should issue a family gathering of all Irishmen in around-table conference[95]

The *Journal* also noted a resolution passed in the P.H. Pearse Sinn Féin Club:

> That we, the members of the P.H. Pearse Sinn Féin Club, of the city of Derry, in public meeting assembled, do hereby pledge ourselves to resist, if necessary, to the domination of any Parliament governing from Belfast, and that a copy of this resolution be sent to the press

As violence continued unabated in Belfast with the birth of the new parliament, the idealism of the Pearse Sinn Féin club did not translate into military activity. In Derry, life was occupied more with the numerous strikes and trade union problems: Watts' Distillery continued to be crippled by a dispute over union recognition, while the carters stopped work once again over pay conditions. The price of commodities was of more concern to nationalists than ways to remove the British army and the 'Specials'. It was not until December that the city saw any IRA activity again. In the first instance, two police constables were killed during a botched jailbreak, and Clooney barracks in the Waterside area was attacked. The attempted jailbreak had repercussions for Collins in Dublin and the RIC in the newly established state of Northern Ireland. Three men were sentenced to hang for their part in the attempted breakout, but on Collins' instructions a rescue squad was assembled under Major General Dan Hogan in January 1922 and sent to Derry. Much to Collins's embarrassment, they were arrested by the USC in Dromore, Co. Down. All were carrying weapons, and it was not until the release, on Collins' orders, of Orangemen who had been kidnapped along the new border, that the Derry prisoners and General Hogan saw their freedom, too.[96] For the RIC, as it was rumoured that a prison officer or warder was involved in the failed prison escape, it gave the new unionist regime in Belfast ammunition to talk about disloyal catholics within the regime. Indeed, on 7 December, the *Journal* quoted William Coote MP as saying that the Special Constabulary would take control of the Derry gaol until there was a 'revision' of the warders.[97] Another incident occurred on 16 March that strained relations between Belfast and Dublin further. The 'Specials' and the RUC seized weapons and a Crossley tender from Free State soldiers who were arrested in Coshquinn, just inside the border on the Londonderry side, while attempting to buy drink in a public house.[98] Those arrested were William McCloskey, Patrick Lee, Charles Coll, Edward Gallagher, Charles Zammitt, Owen Sharkey and William Sherrin.[99] McCloskey spoke on behalf of the defendants and referred to them as being soldiers of the IRA (national army of the Free State). Although they did not recognize the court, McCloskey said they wanted to cooperate as they had crossed the border accidentally. When the soldiers went on trial in September, they were recognizing the legitimacy of the court. Whether this was to obtain a release after being incarcerated for several months, or whether this coincided with the Free State's revised policy on the North in the light of Collins' death, is open to debate. What was important was how it was perceived in Belfast. Home Affairs said the important issue at stake was one of policy, as it was noted that the soldiers who were arrested 'recognised the court and were defended by counsel'.[100]

Although this book is not concerned with the Treaty debates of December 1921 and January 1922, it should be noted that when the split in the IRA occurred in the Free State in 1921, the six northern counties were not exempt from repercussions. Indeed, much has been written on how the ensuing civil war in the Free State split the northern divisions of the IRA depriving them of a united front in the face of unionist hostility and political violence.[101] In Derry, many IRA men who took the side of the anti-Treaty forces moved to Donegal and saw action there throughout 1921 and early 1922. For those that stayed loyal to Collins and HQ in Dublin, the only option was also a trip to

Donegal to fight with the Free State army (against the anti-Treaty forces) or remain in Derry and hope that the Boundary Commission – established between Dublin and London to fix the border of Northern Ireland with the Irish Free State at a later stage – would remove the city from unionism's net, giving it back to Dublin. How impotent republicans had become can be gauged from ideas circulating on how to take the war to the British in the Six Counties. The use of poisonous gas was considered in February 1922. Correspondence received by Shiels from HQ in Belfast shows how cyanide gas could be made. Belfast concluded by saying, 'If you should (think) this is worth any further consideration and desire further details, I will be pleased to let you have them.'[102] It is also interesting to note that during the extensive arrest operation of May 1922, the *Journal* quoted the Press Association saying that additional documents were found concerning poisonous gas in Derry, and that in some cases, 'Specials' involved in the arrests wore gas masks.[103] Until May, with the exception of incidents in March and April, Derry saw little in the way of serious IRA activity. Many members had gone to Donegal to fight with either the Free State army or the Irregulars, while the authorities in and around the city itself seemed to have the upper hand.

The year 1922 saw Belfast burn while James Craig and Michael Collins met (on two occasions) to resolve the political situation. Indeed, there was little let up in the campaign against 'disloyal subjects' and, when the IRA killed David Twaddell MP on 19 May, Craig used this to move against whatever nationalist political base remained.[104] It was also reported that the IRA in Ballyronan, Co. Londonderry, killed two members of the USC in early April: Special Constable Hunter, whose father was the caretaker in the Guildhall, and Special Constable Heggarty, originally from Ferguson's Lane in the city, died when several men ambushed them.[105] The three killings coincided with the arrest of many catholics by the USC under powers bestowed upon it by the Special Powers Act (Northern Ireland) 1922. One author stated that the arrests initiated over the weekend of 20–22 May decimated nationalist and republican thought, leaving the minority population without political direction for many years to come.[106]

The Belfast parliament proscribed the IRA on 22 May. Local newspapers noted that, in the massive round-up, 14 men were arrested in the city itself and over 50 in the county. Many more catholic houses were subjected to searching. Some of the Derrymen arrested included: James Campbell, de Burgh Terrace; James Horner, Mountjoy Terrace;[107] Seamus Cavanagh, Alexander Place; John McLaughlin, Waterloo Street; P. Friel, Nelson Street; three brothers called Mackey; and Captain Charles McGuinness, Argyle Terrace, who was already well-known to the authorities.[108] Horner was captured after he had evaded the original search party.[109] The *Journal* noted that the Mackey brothers and Friel were subsequently released, but another man, Charles MacWhinney, a protestant, was also detained. (It was noted that he was a science teacher in the Technical School.)[110] By the end of May, another 19 battalions of the British army had been deployed to the six counties.

In June, James Murray from Cable Street was shot dead by 'Specials' when a bullet fired at a man after curfew pierced Mr Murray's bedroom window. Several Derry-bound trains were raided in Donegal, and local newspapers reported the bombardment of the Four Courts in Dublin, the first shots in a bitter civil war that was to last until summer 1923. Train raids were becoming ever more frequent, a situation that had not gone unnoticed in Belfast. The protection of the Derry–Strabane line was seen by Colonel Spender, Minister for Home Affairs, to be as important as the neutral zone in the Pettigo–Belleek salient in Co. Fermanagh.[111] Major General Sally-Flood, special military advisor to the Northern Ireland parliament, believed it necessary to 'enter the Free State Territory in order to protect the Railway and Commerce of the country which the Free State Government have failed to do.'[112] Sally-Flood also suggested that the 'military … be allowed to advance to the Line, Letterkenny, Ballybofey, Donegal'. The Ministry of Commerce also pressed hard for the protection of the railway by British troops, saying that they had 'no difficulty in having a Neutral Zone established', but worried that troops used for this purpose could not be used to protect towns like Strabane. The ministry was keen to use the newly established Royal Ulster Constabulary (regular police force created to replace the RIC in the new six-county state) more effectively. On 29 June, the *Belfast Newsletter* carried a short piece saying that the 'strip of Free State territory between Derry and Strabane through which the Great Northern Railway runs will be occupied by British Troops'. However, the publication of this annoyed Spender as it inferred that not all of his conversations were private. By mid-July, after extensive debate and despite the largest train raid yet at Churchill, Co. Donegal (12 July), Home Affairs concluded that 'the Minister is of [the] opinion that the matter (Sally-Flood's plan to invade Donegal) need not be pursued further at present'.[113]

More catholics were arrested in July (Patrick McLaughlin, Samuel Canning, John Doherty and John McGowan) and the Twelfth celebration was marked by extensive revolver firing and curfew breaking: 'the display, which was intended to usher in the twelfth of July celebration, was obviously carried out in utter disregard of Curfew regulations.'[114] July also saw the first deaths of Derry men as a result of fighting in Donegal between Free State troops and IRA Irregulars. William Browne, Bishop Street, died at Derry Infirmary after being brought there by 'Specials' to receive treatment. This led to an important incident involving other Derry IRA men who were now operating in Donegal. Albert Devine, of Brooke Street Avenue, was killed along with another soldier at Glenties when a man dressed as a parish priest tricked them. At his funeral in Derry over 2,000 attended, despite the appearance of a party of Special Constables that caused great anxiety to the mourners, according to the *Journal*. On 2 August, the *Journal* reported that James McCann, a Derry man and leading figure in the Irregulars in Donegal, was captured. He had given himself up after it was reported that the manner of Private Devine's killing had caused the hardcore of his force to break up. It was apparent that anti-Treaty activity in Donegal, which was driven in many instances by Derry men, was soon to peter out. There were also reports that Patrick Shiels and John Fox had gone on hungerstike in Raphoe in protest at their conditions, while the *Journal* reported that James Craig had gone to London to discuss with Westminster the implications for the Six Counties of the Boundary Commission.[115] But the two most striking events of the month occurred many miles from Derry. Arthur Griffith, president of the Free State and negotiator of the Treaty, died on 12 August, and on Friday 25 August the *Journal* reported the death of Michael Collins under the headline 'The Slain Chief'. Its editorial concluded: 'the cause of the tragedy, too poignant almost for tears, is indeed, enmity that is unnatural as it is un-National'. A mass was celebrated for Collins on 4 September in St Eugene's cathedral, with the *Journal* saying that 'the music of the mass was appropriately rendered by the Cathedral Choir. Handel's "Largo" and Beethoven's "Funeral March" were played on the organ.'

With the death of Griffith and Collins, most commentators believed that the Six Counties' chance of rejoining its southern neighbours in the Free State evaporated. Indeed, a memo sent to Dublin by Seamus Woods, then an IRA commander in Belfast, stated that he could detect 'a marked change in some members of GHQ' to the Northern problem since Collins' death, and it was apparent that Dublin was revising its northern policy and deciding that fighting the British authorities in the Six Counties was a task they could not consider any further – particularly since they were now in the midst of a civil war themselves.[116] Hugh C. O'Doherty encapsulated the futility of resistance at a corporation meeting when he said, in a reply to Councillor Robert McAnaney's request for a military post to be removed from Castle Gate: 'times are such that the military and the guns, not this council at all, speak in the city of Derry'.[117] By December, general headquarters in Dublin was stating that 1st and 2nd Northern Divisions, which had previously been amalgamated, were now to be stood down 'and communications are not to be sent to them until further notice'.[118] Indeed, the stomach for the fight to retake the Six Counties was not there. It was shown by the acceptance of the Treaty by the people at elections in June 1922 but more eloquently by the national army's director of chemicals in March 1922:

> Since the publication of the peace terms and the subsequent debates in An Dáil I have lost all interest in the country and am absolutely devoid of any wish to sacrifice myself [in] any way whatsoever for this …

> country. I look upon the above matter [appointment as director] now simply in the light of a job and while believing the Republican Party right I am too selfish to make any sacrifice on their behalf.[119]

With many of its key men behind bars in the Six Counties (James Moore, James Kavanagh, William Cullen, Thomas O'Gara, Michael Devlin and James McCafferty) and further numbers detained in the Free State, IRA activity in Derry was non-existent after August 1922. Many catholics in Derry, as in other parts of the border, were happy to revert back to constitutional politics and hope that the Boundary Commission would deliver their ultimate goal. But as history has shown, this was not to be. On 4 January 1923, the *Sentinel* reported that 'the Dawn of 1923 found the streets of Londonderry deserted save for the "B" Special patrols, Curfew keeping indoors all those who by watchnight services and in other ways usually signal the passing of the Old and the arrival of the New [Year].'[120] The arrival of the new in this instance heralded isolation – some of it imposed, some self-inflicted – for nationalists in Derry and throughout the Six Counties, and many IRA members simply melted into the background, moving to the Free State on their release from prison, be it 1923, 1924 or 1925, or emigrating from Ireland altogether. Indeed, the final word could be left to the USC. When a dinner was held to honour the men and officers of South East Battalion, Hawkins Street (their operational headquarters was called 'Whitehall') in February 1923, the *Sentinel* remarked that this particular unit 'was the battalion which did the most spade work of the force in the most troublous time in Londonderry'.[121] Among many of its members were corporation councillors, some of them the same people that Alderman Meenan would accuse of being responsible for the trouble in June 1920.[122] The newly elected mayor of Derry, Captain Irving-Moore, concluded in his after-dinner speech: 'the Specials, and the "B's" in particular, had been the salvation of Ulster'.

4. The corporation

The election of a combined Sinn Féin-Nationalist corporation for Derry in January 1920 was a complete shock to unionism. As Michael Farrell noted, 'the Derry City result was crucial. Derry held a central place in Orange mythology'.[1] Derry city was important strategically and economically to the well-being of the new Six-County state. This was subsequently illustrated in 1923 when an official from the Northern Ireland Department of Commerce, apropos the city's inclusion in the Free State, noted that 'it would be hampered with Customs formalities in its trade with Northern Ireland and with Great Britain and its trade with these places is beyond doubt the source of its life'.[2] What was more important, a point that Farrell was specifically making, concerned the role the city played during the Williamite wars of the 17th century. Then protestant citizens withstood a major siege on the walled city in 1689 which gave it a symbolic quality. For this reason, it became a potent symbol for the Orange Order and protestantism when the home rule campaign developed in the 1880s.[3] If unionism lost the city now, the moral justification for having a six-county state would have little foundation.

In his inaugural speech the new mayor, Hugh C. O'Doherty, spoke of accommodation and how the corporation would operate to benefit both communities. Alderman Cathal Bradley, of Sinn Féin, said, 'the man elected should be a man possessed of a broad, generous, and – particularly at this time – tolerant outlook'.[4] Indeed, although the mayor's speech was confusing, he made it clear that the city would be administered to benefit both communities.[5] One of the first items addressed was the flying of the Union Jack on corporation property, specifically the Guildhall, which was the seat of local power. The new corporation banned the flying of this flag, but, to maintain a sense of equilibrium, it extended the ban to all political flags, the Irish Tricolour included. To the objective observer, this may have seemed a compromise, but to local unionists it was an insult. The local nationalist newspaper, the *Derry Journal*, did not seem to believe that the new system would accommodate a population eager to maintain the link with London: 'to-day, with the aid of the score of sturdy Nationalists recently invested by the voters under the P.R. system with the status of Corporators, the Gordian knot that remained untied for centuries has been cut'.[6] Evidence is ample that Derry's nationalists were intent on facilitating accommodation, but they too, like their colleagues in Dublin, took the simplistic view that unionism would see a future in a new independent state.

Corporation business for the next few years would evolve around several main platforms: first, there was the ongoing problem of electricity supply which continued to hamper the growth of the city's shipbuilding industry; secondly, there was the issue of the Derry Port & Harbour bill; thirdly, the development of an adequate water supply; and lastly, the twin pillars of education and national allegiance would show that Derry's agenda was not always that of the new Dáil Éireann.

The hope that the city itself would grow came within the boundary of the Port & Harbour bill as well as the extension of the electoral area under the Borough Funds Act of 1888, legislation that the old unionist corporation had developed over several years.[7] However, the new corporation immediately opposed the direction this legislation originally took, primarily because of the new boundaries being proposed. To the corporation, this section would only confirm the gerrymander that existed prior to the PR system that elected them in January 1920.[8] But Derry simply could not ignore the political picture, for, as the country descended into war, the larger issue of loyalty and political jurisdiction inevitably consumed its day-to-day business. In March, as signs emerged that the War of Independence was reaching its streets, the corporation began to show signs of tribal identity. At the monthly meeting on 15 March, Councillor Robinson, on a point of order regarding a debate on partition, said that the chamber in the past had never discussed politics and that they should not start now. The mayor responded: 'I have only to look on this council and ask how it came to be constituted to answer the point of order.'[9] Such motions would always be carried as nationalists held a majority. The issues of partition, education and national allegiance would dominate future sessions.

The adoption of a revised scheme under the Port & Harbour bill was completed in April 1920 just as the city descended into bitter fighting between nationalists and unionists. To date these riots have been seen as sectarian, and although there is an element of truth in this description, again this ignores the wider picture. Economically, the city remained under the control of local unionists, who in turn were mainly protestant. Since the greater proportion of the city's nationalists who sought change were catholic, it followed that political riots would occur along religious lines. Whether such rioting was the work of individuals who did not want the political status of the city to change is open to question, but to dismiss them as sectarian is misleading. In the face of the April disturbances, the mayor when speaking of the members in the chamber said:

> They cannot disguise from themselves that there existed in the city, as in all cities of any size, a rough element which it was impossible for anyone to influence … In addition to these very young people there was a further element of grown men and women who should have sense.[10]

Interestingly, another alderman, Patrick Meenan, who was described by a confidential Dáil report as a moderate nationalist, made the point that every time riots occurred 'raids for weapons took place in nationalist areas and not unionist areas'. As tension increased in the chamber as a result of actions outside, the corporation approved the redistribution of electoral wards to expand the boundaries. Councillor Robinson expressed his disappointment that Alderman Doherty 'had not seen his way to prepare a scheme which the unionists could have adopted. It was obvious from this scheme that its object was to give the nationalists a permanent majority in the corporation.' (Robinson, on the other hand, had no problem endorsing the situation prior to 1920 when the unionist minority maintained power over the city's catholic majority.) The motion was carried on a party vote by 21 to 15.[11]

As stated, the initial trouble in the city in April coincided with the approval by the corporation to seek an expansion of the electoral boundaries (this was partly driven to offset the of previous acts of gerrymandering). The meeting, held on Monday 19 April, followed fierce rioting on Saturday evening (debate in the corporation chamber paralleled by trouble outside was a common feature). Another motion passed concerned the treatment of prisoners in Mountjoy gaol, Dublin:

> The harrowing details of the treatment of political prisoners in Mountjoy Jail shocks the conscience of all civilized peoples. We hereby protest against such treatment and demand that all untried prisoners, against whom no charge has been laid, be discharged, and that all prisoners convicted of political offences be recognised as political prisoners and treated as such. Further, we extend our sympathy to the relatives of our respected townsmen in the cruel ordeal to which they are subjected.[12]

Within three days of the proposal to remove Lord French's name from the city's roll of freemen, serious rioting occurred, this time on Saturday 15 May. The Derry Port & Harbour bill, which was inextricably linked with the Extension bill to redefine the electoral boundaries, was again debated on 21 June, the day that saw the fiercest fighting in the city. Sir Henry Miller (town clerk) said that 'in order for the whole bill to go through as an unopposed measure a proviso should be included giving the minority of the corporation or the electors the right after the next census of appealing to the Local Government Board for a reconsideration of the allocation of members to the various wards.'[13] This illustrates that Miller was quite happy to see a system of gerrymandering operate, and it shows that the next census would only reaffirm what he already knew – that the city's catholic population continued to be in the majority. During the debate, the mayor reported to the corporation the findings of the committee in London. These referred to the petition that Miller sought: it was to be 'disallowed' (although it came from the ratepayers, the majority of whom were protestant) and contained the astonishing remark that the bill

> was a very proper one, and that the extension was very reasonable, in fact too reasonable, and while they were at it they should have taken a larger extension; and that it would have been in the interest of the city, of the Rural District Council, and of the County Council if they had done so.[14]

On hearing that the committee on the bill referred to previous councils as 'Orange', Councillor McCully remarked: 'you (the mayor) should have put the Chairman right when he used that word. It only showed his ignorance. I might as well call you a Ribbon man'. Alderman Meenan quickly replied: 'It would be an honour to him if he was.' The corporation was in the middle of the most important months of its three-year stint. Although unity was maintained in the face of unionist opposition, the alliance between the Nationalists and Sinn Féin was at times an uneasy one. O'Doherty had seen this as a perfect opportunity to show to Ireland and Britain that co-operation could be possible. Indeed, his drive to change the city's electoral boundaries was indicative of this, as were his plans to improve the supply of electricity and water. One of the most ambitious proposals before the corporation was the Banagher waterworks; the tender process for this scheme – proposed by the nationalist Alderman Bonner and seconded by the unionist Councillor Hamilton – was approved at the same meeting that saw Lord French removed from the roll of freemen.

Before long, however, the mayor would face hostility from Dáil Éireann in Dublin as his ambitious plans for cross-community co-operation and advancement of the city's catholics would clash with the greater goal of Dublin's pursuit of national independence.

As mentioned earlier, some of the most important debates concerning legislative change coincided with periods of bitter street fighting. Several councillors believed that some corporation members were responsible for such fighting, but they gave little evidence except to point to the absence of a particular member from the chamber at the time of fighting. In July, when the mayor was explaining London's dilemma over the boundary extension and Port & Harbour bill, Alderman Meenan used the occasion to label unionists who were absent from the meeting on 21 June – when serious trouble occurred – as co-conspirators with the UVF. Alderman Meenan also blamed unionist members for leading the working classes into the affair. However, Councillor Greenway said the employers were not responsible, while Councillor McAnaney, another Sinn Féin member, said the 'affair was concocted by the Ulster Volunteers and the Dorset regiment, acting under the one password which was rumoured to be "Scotland" or "Ulster Volunteer"'.[15]

Interestingly, Councillor J.G. Magee, a unionist, said that he 'did not think it was possible to say with absolute certainty who started the trouble'.[16] A motion condemning the role of the British authorities was also passed:

> The English Government, having failed in the elementary duty which devolves upon all Governments of protecting the lives and property of the people, is hereby denounced for its neglect of duty and called upon to compensate the families of all breadwinners who have lost their lives in the civil turmoil which has taken place in this city and pay compensation to the owners of property for the damage sustained by them from the same cause.[17]

The mayor referred to the deployment of the Irish Volunteers who did their best to stop the looting and burning of property and referred to the 'fifteen or twenty protestants who were manly enough to come out and thank them for their protection'. On Wednesday morning the Guildhall Tower had union jacks flying from it in defiance of the ban on flying flags, and many shops had anti-catholic graffiti splashed on their windows and doors, while the mayor's residence in Bayview Terrace was defaced with 'God save the King' as was the entrance to the Guildhall itself. In the evening, during a sitting of the corporation, a police constable came – brandishing a revolver – and warned members not to remove union flags that were put up on the Guildhall; he quickly left when challenged by the assistant town clerk.

The corporation continued to live with a volatile situation. The explosion of violence in Belfast in July did not help matters, which the *Journal* reported under the heading 'Belfast joins Derry in war on catholics'.[18] The lockout of shirt workers continued, while the city had been without street lighting from 1 May as a result of the shortage of coal due to a strike in England.[19]

One major problem that arose out of the destruction of life and property was the question of compensation. The mayor was adamant that London should carry the cost, which ran into thousands of pounds, but some corporation members were not so sure. At its meeting on 21 June, the corporation called on London to take responsibility for compensation claims which were due to arise. However, in Dublin, Dáil Éireann was not in agreement. The provisional government felt that the corporation itself would have to pay compensation and fix its rates accordingly. In August, as the mayor continued to strive for change at a local level, Patrick Shiels, a member of the corporation and an officer in the IRA, wrote to Sinn Féin in Dublin seeking advice. Shiels alleged that, although the mayor had sympathies with Sinn Féin, 'he does not belong to Sinn Féin here and takes no part in the local activities'. He said that O'Doherty was the agreed candidate for the mayor's position as part of a general 'catholic Party' organized to oppose unionism in the city. He continued: 'his policy is largely, if not wholly, mapped out in consultation with the Revd Dr.

McHugh, Bishop of Derry, who is a bitter opponent of Sinn Féin.' In a startling document, he set forth the reasons why they had supported O'Doherty's pursuit of electoral change and the Derry Port & Harbour bill. Not only would it countermand gerrymandering, but also 'the bill contained necessary borrowing powers to help alleviate the financial hardship currently felt by the corporation; and thirdly, it was believed by SF in the City that headquarters did not oppose the Derry branch's course of action.' But confusion had arisen as the mayor was prepared to pay compensation to two RIC officers who had been injured recently in rioting. Shiels also recalled that in a recent conversation with Arthur Griffith, O'Doherty claimed Griffith had said that 'necessary sacrifices should be made to hold the city as long as it did not involve any sacrifice of principle'.[20] O'Doherty, solicitor, constitutional nationalist and former supporter of Charles Stewart Parnell, was now engaged in the most difficult period of his political career. Trying to balance national republican aspirations with local politics in the city, he found himself pleasing no one.

It is clear that there were now divisions within the 'catholic party'. Shiels, as an officer in the IRA, would have realized that the presence of three regiments of British soldiers in the city presented a very difficult obstacle to their campaign, and as a member of the corporation, he would now have realized that a change of policy was called for. The key question he posed was as follows: 'whether, when republican principles and the "welfare of the city" clash owing to whatever cause, we are to allow principle to be set aside on any pretext?'[21] Reaction was swift. Dublin thought it better to avoid confrontation than to split the 'Catholic Party', but on the specific question of republican principle, said: 'on no account must any temporary or permanent benefit to the city be allowed to set aside republican principles'. The letter also claimed that the only direct link to Derry came 'via the mayor's son', whom it claimed was a republican. On the question of the bill currently going through London, the writer said:

> I quite appreciate the financial crux in Derry, and the impossibility of countenancing a bill in Westminster without sacrificing principle. Every Local Authority in Ireland is faced with serious financial embarrassments. It is the duty of Republicans to endeavour to bridge over those troubles by every possible means, and by this I mean without the assistance of the British Government.

On the issue of compensation and the comment allegedly made by Arthur Griffith, the letter was equally emphatic:

> The payment of any decree under Malicious and Criminal Injuries is bad. It is bad in law and against nationalist principles. All over Ireland Councils are declining to pay these decrees. The case against paying

> them is on the highest national grounds. Even one grand Jury passed a resolution that Malicious Injury claims should be paid out of State funds and the action of the Finance Committee in this case is inconceivable. The rest of Ireland is losing money for Housing, Drainage, Tuberculosis (Sanatorium) and every other service for which the Local Taxation Account and other funds are raised. The particular circumstances of any case are no mitigation for sacrificing principle. It appears from the facts disclosed that "necessary sacrifices are being made to hold the city for the enemy and sacrificing every principle to do so.[22]

The fallout from this command continued into September. In an unsigned letter sent to the Minister for Local Government (written on *Young Ireland* headed paper) dated 25 September 1920, one commentator remarked on the advice given to Shiels:

> Your answer seems to me to slightly overlook the importance of holding Derry against the Carsonites. You do not emphasize sufficiently that while upholding rigidly Republican principles, no matter should unnecessarily be introduced that would split the coalition against the Carsonites. I told the mayor "necessary sacrifices of feeling might be made to secure the holding of the city", as long as national principle was not sacrificed.

The writer also alleged that the mayor was being bypassed on matters of policy: the Local Government ministry in Dublin only seemed to communicate with the Sinn Féin branch.[23] The importance of this debate, which took place over two months in 1920, should not be underestimated as it went to the very heart of Derry nationalism. On the one hand, as Shiels rightly pointed out, the mayor was friendly with Bishop McHugh, who in turn saw partition as evil; more importantly, McHugh saw the catholic church losing control of education under a partitioned state.[24] On the other hand, there was the alliance of Sinn Féin members who saw declaring their allegiance to Dáil Éireann as the only hope for the city in the context of the national struggle.

In September, the *Journal* reported that large numbers of compensation claims for damages had been filed against the corporation, while local businesses struggled as a result of the railway strike affecting Ireland generally. The interesting point here, which the mayor alluded to later, concerns the amount of money being claimed and by whom. Since most of the property damaged belonged to ratepayers, and most ratepayers were protestant, it stood that those making claims were protestant. On 18 October, in the aftermath of another weekend of violence, the mayor had this to say about the situation:

> God knows … since I came into the occupation of the chair I have done my level best to preserve the lives and the property of the citizens during the very dangerous times through which we are passing, but unless I have the co-operation of the Unionists of this city, as I have the co-operation of my own co-religionists and co-Nationalists my efforts will fail and for generations to come this city will struggle under a load of debt which will prevent the growth and expansion of the city, cripple its industry, and ruin, above all, the Unionist merchants who are the principal owners of property.[25]

Whether the mayor was deliberately accusing unionist ratepayers of embarrassing him with such claims remains to be seen, but there can be no doubt that this issue drove a wedge between the two wings of the nationalist alliance on the corporation. In the aftermath of trouble on 8 November, when the British army killed Constable Hugh Kearns, the mayor condemned the violence and called for an inquiry into what he saw as the illegal activity of the RIC. Sir John McFarland supported this stance, too; he also called upon the citizens of Derry to form volunteer groups to protect property: 'every man had a right to assist in the protection of his own property. The citizens should combine and take joint action, and by these means trouble to a large extent could be averted.'[26]

As Christmas approached, the mayor saw his plans disappear under the imminent policy of partition, dissension within the 'catholic Party', and opposition from Unionism. Although the corporation, as alluded by a London *Times* correspondent in June,[27] strove to be objective in its dealings with the city's population, the war that was now gripping the country overshadowed O'Doherty's dream of improving the city for all citizens, but in particular, its catholic citizens.

When he was re-elected mayor in January 1921, partition was a reality. But he continued to speak optimistically when referring to the corporation: 'the whole body, without distinction, set themselves to administer the affairs of the city in a businesslike and capable manner'. He referred to two particular schemes, the Banagher Water Scheme and the Electrical Light Station, the latter having been completed but the former stalled due to a lack of money. And again, he spoke out about partition.[28] He was also exercised by the closure of the US consular agency in Derry. According to reports in the local newspapers, Washington D.C. had decided that as a result of the economic situation in Derry, all business should be concentrated on the Belfast office. However, the *Journal* quoted the US representative, a man called O'Hagan, as saying the real reason was not to do with economics and he disagreed with the strategy being pursued.[29] As the War of Independence continued nationally, and partition and the creation of the new Northern Ireland was cemented, voices of reason continued to be heard. The Derry harbour board reported a profit for 1920 and its chairman, Mr R. Watson, urged people to look to the future:

> We are now on the eve of great changes in the administration of the affairs of the country, and it was impossible at this stage to say what effect these changes would have in the affairs of the port ... but hope that everyone would recognise that it was in their mutual interests to work harmoniously together and to do everything possible to promote the welfare of the port and increase its popularity with ship owners and others.[30]

Figures for the shipyard were improving, too – the company launched three vessels of 21,200 tons gross, being an increase of 6,879 tons on the previous year – and the outlook for the future was good. In early February, the first general cargo steamer from the United States arrived in the port with the Moore and McCormack Line. Council business continued despite the turbulent atmosphere in the country (rates were struck in February at 17*s.* in the pound, slightly down on the previous year) and many of the sub-committees, particularly the Finance committee, struggled to come to terms with the shortage of coal that continued to affect the city's supplies. Indeed, in April, the Rock Biscuit Company and several shirt factories warned that employment was in jeopardy if coal was not found for a reasonable price.[31] The corporation also struck a new rate to cover compensation as a result of rioting in 1920, adding a further 6*s.* in the pound to the existing rate.[32] Further confrontation was created when the IRA was active, killing one policeman and injuring several others, over the weekend 1–3 April, and notice was served on electors of the first elections under the auspices of the new Northern Ireland regime, with an election pact again favoured by nationalists and Sinn Féin, to maximize the nationalist vote. Michael Collins had approved the policy of contesting elections for the Belfast Parliament (which Sinn Féin did not recognise) in January. In a letter to de Valera, he stated:

> To put forward candidates ... is the only policy consistent with our past action of contesting every seat in Ireland ... From an outside point of view, I greatly fear that refusal to take part in the elections would look like an admission of defeat – would look like the skulking of a schoolboy who got a severe drubbing and had not the decency to recover himself.[33]

Derry city and county returned two Nationalist/Sinn Féin candidates to three Unionists.[34] The *Journal* on 1 June assessed the new state's viability:

> It cannot regulate tax on tea and tobacco, nor alcoholic drink. The Six Counties will have to pay £7,920,000 to Britain. This burden is greater

> than the burden placed on the defeated Germany, which is fifty times the population of Ireland. How will the prosperity of mutilated Ulster survive under three times a greater burden? … That there is nothing in it to "enthuse" over even the duped denizens of Shankill Road must begin to see before long.[35]

Also in June, Watts Distillery agreed to sell 100 tons of coal to the corporation as the shortage became more acute. This gesture came while serious questions were being asked about the distillery's future, as trade union conflict was rampant and sales in traditional markets abroad were falling. The union problem reflected the political situation, as members of the Irish Transport and General Workers' Union (IT&GWU) within the distillery continued to undermine members associated to the British union, NAUL. Again, loyalty reflected political allegiances with many nationalist workers joining the IT&GWU from NAUL. One writer to the *Journal* on 22 June said 'that the IT&GWU drove a wedge between the two unions at the height of violence on June 1920 when it appealed to members to leave the NAUL'. By the middle of the month, the distillery had ceased production as a result of a strike over pay, but the undercurrent of union recognition (with its political implications) was there. By the end of October, Watts had closed its distillery transferring production to Belfast. It was another blow to the local economy.[36]

With the Truce declared in July and violence in Belfast abating for the first time in several months, the political problem of Derry's allegiance was again the focus in the corporation chamber. On 25 August, the most important debate since June 1920 took place, when Alderman Cathal Bradley tabled the following motion:

> That as the majority of the people of Derry City have expressed in election their determined opposition to the so-called Northern Parliament, and have declared that they will refuse to recognise its authority, such authority could only be exercised by force and coercion. We desire to live in union and harmony with all our fellow countrymen, and protest against this calumniating act of British policy, which has sought to divide us in order to dominate us, and which for that purpose has set up an arbitrary, new-fangled, and unnatural boundary, and based neither on the will of the people nor on any other valid ground, historical, geographical, or economical. We refuse to consent to any such separation from the rest of Ireland, and pledge ourselves to oppose it steadfastly and to make the fullest use of our right to nullifying it.[37]

The scene was set for a wide and varied debate on the corporation's attitude to recognising the Belfast parliament or declaring allegiance to Dáil Éireann. The *Journal* carried extensive reporting on the debate in its edition of 26

September. Bradley said that he 'trusted that the resolution would not be regarded by anyone as a reflection on the ability of Ulstermen to govern themselves', and Alderman Richard Doherty, while supporting the resolution, said that 'to have any division of our country will mean the perpetuation of internecine strife and all its deplorable consequences.' In opposing the resolution, Councillor Burns pointed out that the proposal opposed the Northern parliament, one that was already in existence, but more importantly, he referred to Councillor Bradley's resolution to remove Lord French's name from the freemen's roll (that in turn led to rioting).[38] Councillor Greenway said the resolution gave offence to the 'loyalists of Northern Ireland, and in particular, Derry City'. He continued that this resolution would not cause Sir James Craig 'to turn in his sleep'. Interestingly, he made the point: 'we are the chosen few Derry Corporators, and, remembering the old adage, "What cannot be cured must be endured", our business as Corporators was not with outside politics.' It was an admission that the nationalist population of the city knew what lay ahead and that they should learn to come to terms with it. Councillor Logue said that it was ironic that the party Councillor Greenway supported was in opposition to partition and home rule only seven years previously. Councillor Thompson expressed surprise at the announcement, as he did not think the corporation should consider such resolutions. He then added that he did not want separation, he wanted the whole country to remain under the union jack: they had the Six Counties and 'Please God, we will hold them.' Councillor Morris said the motion had been 'mildly proposed but angrily received'; she had been asked not to introduce religion to the debate (by Sinn Féin) but thought that religion was at the root of everything.

The mayor, in a somewhat conciliatory rein, said it was right to ask questions, as partition would have a serious affect on Derry. He said the proposal to partition the country should be opposed on national and economic grounds: 'If all Ulster is given a Parliament after the proposal has been submitted to the Irish people, I will bow to it and do my best to support it. But it must be all Ulster.' The resolution was passed by 22 votes to 15. But it is important to remember that the resolution fell short of declaring the corporation's allegiance to Dublin. The *Journal*, in an editorial, stated:

> By the adoption of the resolution the corporation are not only taking their stand in support of the priceless principle of the preservation of National Unity as an indispensable constituent of just government in Ireland, but they perform a service to their city in the practical sense of no slight value. Derry's material interests have never had sympathetic consideration at partition headquarters if they felt they conflicted ever so slightly with those of Belfast. Sectarian intoleration is not the sole besotting sin of the latter city. Rampant commercial greed has helped to dig the pit into which it has fallen.[39]

In the aftermath of the debate, violence in Belfast erupted once again while President de Valera met a deputation from Fermanagh and Tyrone to discuss the implications of partition. A week later, a deputation from Derry went to Dublin to see de Valera and Erskine Childers, Minister for Propaganda.[40] Such visits were indicative of the time, as Northern nationalists sought reassurance from Dublin that they were not going to be abandoned to the Northern parliament.[41] To show public support for the people of Derry, Eoin MacNeill appeared at St Columb's Hall on 8 September to repudiate Britain's right to interfere in Irish affairs. On 21 September, the corporation debated the issue of riot compensation, with some Sinn Féin members wanting London (and not Derry corporation) to carry the cost of reimbursement, but day-to-day items such as price-fixing, particularly when it came to gas, unemployment, and the amount of work strikes that seemed to affect the city (in September it was the turn of the carters once again) continued to be overshadowed by political developments. By December, Derry's fate, as that of the other six counties, was sealed. On 7 December, the *Journal* noted the establishment of the Free State and in its editorial two days later stated: 'excellent as it appeared at the first view, the Treaty further improves on closer acquaintance. One sees the full extent of its carrying power only on the fourth or fifth reading of its terms.' The stance of the paper was at odds with that taken by the mayor who only saw the Treaty as copper fastening partition. With this in mind another Northern deputation met de Valera, this time on 9 December, but these were more difficult times as the president had now decided that the terms on offer were not acceptable to him. This was another watershed for Derry's nationalist corporation, as not only did it show diversity within the opinion of Derry nationalists themselves, but also the difficulty inherent in Northern nationalism in general, a theme explored by Eamon Phoenix. Although the meeting took place over 8 and 9 December in the Mansion House, it was clear prior to this date that de Valera would not accept the terms of the Treaty.[42] What was conspicuous by its absence, as far as the Northern delegation was concerned, was the issue of partition. They were more concerned with the issues of proportional representation and education, two important issues they saw disappearing in the Northern parliament. Astonishingly, the mayor of Derry proposed that the nine counties of Ulster should come under a Belfast parliament that would, in turn, safeguard their rights:

> Some of the arguments we have heard seem to proceed on the basis of diminution of the area. Now, if the area is diminished [or] if it is left as it is in the six counties the minority will never have any voice in the control of that area, no matter what safeguards there are, and there will be the same monopolising by the Orange Ascendancy crowd as in the past ... A subordinate parliament for all Ulster, that would give such a representation to the minority in the Belfast Parliament, together with

> Labour, as would give them a chance of having control at the same time, unless the minority have a chance of coming into power at some time in this area no man of standing or reputation in the reserved area of Ulster will think it worth his while to go into Parliament. If you brought in all Ulster you would create such a strong Parliament that you would give us some chance. That, Mr President, with proportional representation would secure us in all our rights.[43]

Archie Savage, a Sinn Féin member from East Belfast, asked the mayor whether he would envisage such a state under an English or Irish State, and O'Doherty replied: 'within an Irish State, of course'. Another member, Michael Lynch, said that it was only in Derry that such an idea had been mooted, whereas in the rest of Ulster there was a belief that there should be no Northern parliament. De Valera continued to speak about the situation being unresolved – 'Nothing is settled' – to which O'Doherty asked: 'Do I understand you to say that under this scheme as it stands, Dáil Éireann will have all powers? If that is so, a great deal of our objections will be met.' President de Valera replied: 'That is, in other words, they would say, are you going to have all the patronage. Even in that Instrument you have not any agreement as regards the law or finance. The whole question of the North is left open.' Interestingly, in the light of his pronouncements over the Treaty and his subsequent anti-Treaty stance, de Valera had no objection to Derry recognizing An Dáil.[44]

Sinn Féin in the city was not long in taking up the cudgel. On 22 December four Sinn Féin members drafted the following resolution and sent it to the town clerk and Mayor O'Doherty:

> Whereas the City of Derry for reason of its economic and geographical position and of the wishes of its inhabitants is entitled to be included in the Parliament of the Irish Free State and whereas this corporation has already repudiated allegiance and connection with the parliament of 'Northern Ireland', we, the corporation of Derry City, thoroughly representative of the citizens and acting in their best interests, hereby pledge our allegiance to Dáil Éireann and shall endeavour to the best of our ability to ensure that our city shall take its rightful place in the parliament of the majority of the Irish people[45]

Bishop McHugh, in advance of its being brought before the corporation in January 1922, sent a copy of the resolution to MacNeill in Dublin. McHugh was worried about sectarian tension in the city if such a resolution was passed: 'in my mind the action of these people [Sinn Féin members] in present circumstances is sheer madness. The mayor will not call the meeting or 28th inst. as requested, but those who signed the requisition may persist in having such meeting later on.'[46] If such a course was pursued, he continued, 'in Derry now we would have neither catholic mayor nor catholic corporation to present our case to the Boundary Commission.' The bishop was confident that the motion would be defeated, and showing contempt for the resolution and Sinn Féin in general, concluded:

> It is really too bad that a few individuals should be allowed to run amok like this and jeopardise for all time the interests of nearly 30,000 catholics in this city. You should take steps to stop the foolish action of these people and in my opinion if necessary you should come here at once as you are said member for both city and Co. Derry.

There is no evidence that MacNeill replied to this letter. Indeed, the establishment of a National Academy of Ireland seemed to occupy him more in those early months of 1921 rather than the plight of Derry's nationalist population – the city he had been elected to serve.[47] On 1 January 1922, the *Journal* reported that the Owen Roe O'Neill Band Club had carried a motion calling on the corporation to recognize Dáil Éireann, and this was quickly followed in their edition of 4 January when a letter, published under the name 'Vigilante', asked why the corporation had not declared its allegiance to Dublin: 'beyond passing a negative resolution repudiating allegiance to the Belfast Parliament, the City Council has done nothing.' Prior to the vote on 10 January, Alderman Meenan replied to the request from 'Vigilante'. In a letter published two days later, he asked how the corporation could recognize something that did not exist (an Irish Free State which had not been approved by Dáil Éireann as yet). He continued: 'from an Ulsterman's point of view the settlement is nothing to boost of–in my view it puts us in a worse position than we would have been if the Lloyd George proposals of 1916 had been accepted and put into operation'. Again, this prompted the motion, signed by Hegarty, Cathal Bradley, Anthony Carlin and Michael Cosgrove, which stated:

> Whereas the City of Derry for reason of its economic and geographical position and of the wishes of its inhabitants is entitled to be included in the Parliament of the Irish Free State and whereas this Corporation has already repudiated allegiance and connection with the parliament of 'Northern Ireland', we, the Corporation of Derry City, thoroughly representative of the citizens and acting in their best interests, hereby pledge our allegiance to Dáil Eireann and shall endeavour to the best of our ability to ensure that our city shall take its rightful place in the parliament of the majority of the Irish people.[48]

This triggered a series of bitter accusations and counter-accusations that were played out in the letters' pages of the *Derry Journal* over the next few weeks.

When the motion was brought before the corporation on 10 January, it was ruled out of order.[49] With the Treaty ratified by a small majority in Dublin on 7 January, both Sinn Féin clubs in the city subsequently repudiated the stance taken at the meeting and in particular that of the mayor, Hugh C. O'Doherty:

> Arising out of the mayor's action in the passing of the malicious injuries rate under the alleged authority of Dáil Éireann and the ruling out of motion of allegiance to Dáil Éireann, and in face of his recent public statement that the corporation should recognise the Northern Parliament, thereby breaking the election pledge given in 1919 to the people of Derry, and also the resolution of non-recognition placed on the minutes of the Council, we, the members of ... hereby call on the Republican members of the corporation to abstain in future from all co-operation with avowed partitionists.[50]

They were declaring their allegiance to de Valera and the policy of Sinn Féin. The first signs of a serious split in Derry were now in the open. In tandem, the Belfast Boycott, which had been running for many months, but with little coördinated support in Derry itself, was called off on 25 January.

By not declaring his allegiance to Dublin, while repudiating Belfast's authority, the mayor fell between two policies and pleased no one. He isolated the Sinn Féin contingent of the 'catholic Party' with the former stance, while he alienated the unionist camp with his stance towards Belfast. He saw his salvation in the Boundary Commission, which although written into the Treaty terms under Article 12, had yet to be accepted by James Craig. Another delegation travelled to Dublin on Saturday 6 February, this time to meet with Michael Collins who had recently met James Craig in January for the first time. Collins reaffirmed his commitment to their anti-partition cause, but his policy muddled through the months of April, May and June, as he grappled with a deteriorating domestic situation that would culminate with civil war in July. As early as 10 April the *Journal* quoted Collins saying that a civil war could only be averted by a miracle.[51] In an earlier edition the *Journal* argued that such a split would be disastrous for the Six Counties: 'a split in Ireland means the despair of the Irish people; it means more emigration; it means an extension of Carsonism into more Irish soil. A fratricidal war between Irish Republicans and Irish Free Staters would leave Ireland desolate: only Britain would benefit by suicidal strife.'[52]

As this developed nationally, in the city itself the mayor grappled with the continuing problem of who should administer the port and maintain the bridge. A proposal before the corporation to have the Port & Harbour bill passed by the Belfast parliament (the bill itself was based on the earlier Corporation bill of 1921) would enable the corporation to obtain additional powers in connection with the bridge's maintenance and running. Sir Henry

Miller proposed to increase to £4000 the amount that the harbour commissioners could call upon from each corporation per year while initiating discussions on the eventual transfer of power. Con Doherty said that he would agree with the town clerk as the commissioners 'had neglected their trust and the state of the bridge was a disgrace to the citizens, who were blamed for it'. The mayor then alluded to the dilemma before them:

> I agree that the corporation was the body that should have control of the bridge. Now a position had arisen that was somewhat difficult. If a government were legislating in Ireland in which the people of all sections had confidence undoubtedly it would be their duty to promote a bill to take over the bridge ... What action should I take?

Councillor Morris replied,'No action'. The mayor was introducing the sphere of politics to the debate, something that Councillor Magee on previous occasions bitterly disagreed with:'we are not here for political purposes, but to do the best we can for the community'. The mayor's motion of not to do anything was seconded by Councillor Hegarty. Sir John McFarland asked the mayor to reconsider, as it would leave the citizens paying two thirds of the rates (estimated to be 1*s.* in the pound) and the Commissioners would simply continue on with the bill. Councillor Bonner replied that there are two reasons against the amendment: firstly, the Bridge Commissioners would be dissolved in a few weeks and secondly, the Boundary Commission: it had not determined whether Derry City would be in Northern or Southern Ireland. The mayor's motion was passed.

Again, Belfast continued to make the news as the number of dead continued to rise in the war between USC and the British army on the one side, and a loose coalition of pro-Treaty and anti-Treaty IRA forces on the other. By May, the city was under a cloud that had not existed since June 1920, with many nationalists being arrested over the weekend 19–22 May under the Special Powers Act. Again, the mayor used the chamber of the corporation to call for calm:

> To my fellow-citizens within the city, I say be patient, one and all. I beg all my Nationalist fellow-citizens to do no act that would provoke a breach of the peace, but to trust the mayor to do all he can, fearless and regardless of the consequences to himself, to maintain this city for Ireland, and if temporarily he thinks it better policy in the interest of all protestants and catholics, to allow this Northern Government to function in his city, then I ask my catholic and Nationalist fellow-citizens not to misunderstand me, but that I do it for one purpose only, and that purpose the good of all and the good of Ireland.[53]

How volatile the situation had become can be gauged by reading the local papers for the months of May and June. There can be no doubt that Craig was under immense pressure in Belfast from his own people, while in Dublin, Collins and the provisional government were waging a war against former colleagues. Casualties mounted on both sides. By July, the North of Ireland Shipbuilding Company had closed its operation as a result of the shortage of electricity, and the corporation infuriated unionists when the majority nationalists overruled a unionist motion of sympathy on the death of Sir Henry Wilson in July.[54] Criticized by the *Sentinel* and *Standard*, Mayor O'Doherty responded: 'Where were their voices [Unionist members of corporation] when the McMahons were murdered?'[55] As Phoenix has noted: 'by 3 June 1922, the end was in sight of offensive action by the pro-treaty IRA in the north. Collins seems to have been influenced by "Devlinite businessmen", MacRory's desire "for an honourable truce" and the abundant evidence that the policy of belligerence had proved fatally counter-productive.'[56]

Within the month both Michael Collins and Arthur Griffith were dead and the new policy in Dublin, under the provisional government now headed by W.T. Cosgrave, was one of retrenchment from the north and consolidation in Dublin. For Derry and other nationalist areas of Northern Ireland, there was no hope of further military intervention since the Civil War pre-occupied the new Dublin administration: the government simply believed that the Boundary Commission would be their salvation. Although the Boundary Commission is outside the scope of this book, it is important to know that 'nationalists ... blithely assumed that, at the very least, they would find Derry handed over to the Free State'.[57] With the abolition of proportional representation in September for local council elections, O'Doherty knew that there would not be another term in office in January 1923. The debate now arose as to whether northern nationalists should take their seats in the Belfast parliament, while unionists set in motion the chain of command for future generations. In October, the medical superintendent of health, Margaret O'Doherty, was requested to take an oath to King George V and the Northern Ireland parliament, a sign of how things would be in the near future for catholics who wanted to remain in such positions.[58] On 2 November 1922, the fate of Derry's claim for inclusion in the Free State was inextricably linked to the future of the Boundary Commission when a conference held in St Columb's Hall, presided over by Fr L. Hegarty, decided not to contest the forthcoming elections in January 1923. The final meeting of the nationalist corporation was held on 9 January 1923. Captain Maxwell Scott Moore JP was subsequently elected mayor for the city on 24 January. It would be another fifty years before another catholic wore the mayoral chain of Derry.[59]

Conclusion

In his New Year message, widely circulated among the unionist press in January 1923, James Craig said:

> I thank everyone for the splendid part they have played in contributing towards the end we in Ulster have attained by their unfailing devotion and loyalty. When I compare the state of our beloved province a short year ago with what it is now, I am filled with unspeakable thankfulness and pray that now that we are on the road to peace everyone will work together in harmony and goodwill towards the restoration of prosperity and endeavour to maintain in the Empire the high repute gained for us by our forefathers.[1]

When the first meeting was held under the guidance of the new Unionist corporation, the *Journal* reported that Councillor Greenway immediately requested the hoisting of the Union Jack (it had only flown once above the Guildhall since 1919) and invoked the memory of Ulster sons who had died in the Great War of 1914–18. But there were dissenting voices. Councillor Robinson said: 'I do not feel it is necessary that any flag or any emblem should be flown from the Guildhall, either from the spire or any other part … in the interests of the peace of the city the unionists should refuse to give offence to any section of the community.' The mayor adjourned the issue until a later date, when Robinson was overruled; his bid for cross-community relations was short-lived.[2]

This book set out to address whether or not nationalist Derry shared the political aims of Dublin while the War of Independence was being fought during 1919–21. In addressing this question, it sought to look at the level of violence initiated by the Irish Volunteers/IRA while monitoring what the corporation did during the relevant period. Indeed, one also has to consider the level of input from Dublin, and Collins directly, to view the overall picture when looking at Derry at the time. At one level, Derry did believe in the cause of Ireland as illustrated by the variety of motions passed by the corporation, but these same motions also illustrate the corporation's limitations, as not one of them overtly declared the city's allegiance to Dáil Éireann. Many of the motions passed in the chamber referred to the corporation's abhorrence of partition; in late 1922, when Belfast was proposing (and enforced) a reversion to electoral boundaries prior to proportional representation, the city again evaded the opportunity to declare for Dáil Éireann. The motion before the corporation simply read: 'we, the corporation of the County and City of Derry, representing the majority of the Inhabitants of said City, hereby re-iterate our protest against the partition of Ireland and the setting up of a Parliament for Six Counties thereof in Belfast. We further protest against the arrangement of the Wards in this City made by the Belfast Parliament for the purpose of depriving the majority of the City of their just rights.'[3] When it came to making momentous political decisions, the thought of lives being lost as a result of policy loomed large, and the nationalist members – but in particular the mayor – decided they had no authority to risk the lives of the city's citizens. There is no evidence that the corporation gave its allegiance to Dáil Éireann, publicly or privately, as councils in Fermanagh and Tyrone had done previously. Indeed, the authorities in Belfast abolished Fermanagh county council as a result of this and appointed a commissioner to administer its affairs.[4] Perhaps Derry was aware of such an outcome, with Mayor O'Doherty prudent in his actions given the state of affairs that existed locally. He had hoped the Boundary Commission would deliver the city to the Free State, but this option all but disappeared when Belfast abolished proportional representation for local elections in September 1922. Why he did not react then is unknown, and until such evidence is found to show differently it can be assumed he fell short of the goal of national republican principle. In the aftermath of fighting in the Beleek-Pettigo area in Fermanagh, May 1922, and having been harassed himself by the USC, the mayor made an impassioned plea at a corporation meeting:

> I do not wish it said that when history comes to report the extra-ordinary events that are occurring around us that during the occupancy of this chair by the first catholic mayor of Derry that this old and ancient city, that traces its origins back to St Columbkille, which many an historic incident has happened, has been destroyed. I do not wish it to be said that when I leave this chair that this city is in ruins.[5]

There can be no doubt that the weight of history sat heavily on O'Doherty's shoulders in these months. The city itself had seen many killed, wounded, and expelled while both the IRA and British forces had destroyed property as a result of their actions. In an editorial mid-1922, the *Journal* said 'it would seem that all hope may be abandoned that the partition Government of Belfast have any intention of dealing out even-handed justice in checking the fierce onslaughts on Nationalists that are being made from day to day'.[6] In the light of this, the mayor and the nationalist corporation grappled with uncertainty, high levels of military activity, and the prospect of retaliation by the unionist community that was now formalized under the umbrella of the USC and sanctioned in the defence of the new state.[7] This latter point must be left open to debate as evidence and folklore continue to overlap concerning the role of the USC and the wider unionist community during this, the 'troubled period'.[8] Indeed, as recently as 2001 David Trimble MP rejected allegations that the USC were involved in such killings.[9] Eighty-two years later and stones remain unturned.

When elected, there can be no doubt that the mayor believed there was a golden opportunity to rectify past ills and expand the city to benefit the community as a whole. He said as much in his maiden speech to the corporation. Although the speech was contradictory, it should be read in the context of the time: he was the first catholic in Derry in modern times to hold such a position, and the elation which this brought may have pushed him to be more nationalistic than he perhaps wanted to be. Indeed, his own experience (as a solicitor and member of the IPP) would not have equipped him to deal with the violence, uncertainty and political indecision that developed through 1920 and 1921, culminating with the barring of the Sinn Féin motion that declared allegiance to Dáil Éireann in January 1922. In the end, this brought closure on the political debate on the position of Derry itself in the context of republican principle. In Dublin, as early as May 1922, it was obvious that Dáil Éireann would now accept the partitioning of the country that was first accepted by the IPP in 1916. An incomplete memo called 'Memorandum of the Northern Question' stated: 'in regard to the question of coercion by force, it is best to say very little. It must be remembered that we have the pledge of the British Government that the whole resources of the British Empire would be at the disposal of Ulster in resisting any compulsion of that nature.'[10] It is difficult to know if Collins or Desmond FitzGerald, who was then Minister for Publicity, specifically held this view, but it is indicative of the attitude at the time.

Within three months, government policy publicly changed with consolidation inside the Free State replacing any lingering concerns over the plight of Northern nationalists, even though for much of late 1921 and early 1922 anti-partition speeches were frequently made for public consumption. Derry's local policy concerns, which in many ways conflicted with Dublin in September 1921, marked a reversal of fortunes on how the city was viewed by its southern brethren. The view that northern policy died with Collins is not completely true: as the memo listed above shows, a pro-active policy for the North was dying by May even though Collins continued to ship weapons and munitions in June to the beleaguered counties.[11] As Tim Pat Coogan commented, 'Collins was in an extraordinary delicate situation, pulled between the machinations of de Valera to appeal to the increasingly militant Republicans on the one hand, and the British and Craig on the other.'[12] While Derry's nationalists seethed over the ineffectual protection offered by the RIC and their alleged involvement in murder, Dáil Éireann went about its business of building a nation state.[13] Although the expulsion of catholics in Lurgan and

Portadown had come up again in November 1920, Derry received scant attention in Dáil notes. Fisheries, agriculture and the first signs of a future education policy are seen in the records.[14] The Six Counties, firmly established by mid-1921, were slowly slipping off Dublin's map. Collins' ongoing direction of the Civil War, his involvement in the financing of the general loan and his heavy cabinet responsibilities ensured that Ulster was one battle that could be shelved for another day. Indeed, although he took great interest in Ulster throughout the period February-August 1922, there is no conclusive evidence that a second phase of military activity would have been initiated had he lived.[15]

From the sources consulted for this book, the role of the IRA during the period was very limited in its effectiveness. Augusteijn quotes police sources as saying there were 305 Irish Volunteers in the city by late 1920, but in June of the same year it was alleged in military despatches to Dublin that there were thousands of men available to fight for the city in the aftermath of the killing of catholics on Saturday 19 June.[16] Derry stood at a crossroad: there were many males who had combat experience as a result of the war of 1914–18 and there seems to have been a sufficient supply of weapons. But what happened? By the end of the month, from a situation whereby the IRA had 'absolute control of over 50 per cent of the City area', no effort was made in pursuit of the national republican cause to take the remaining parts of the city. With British army reinforcements arriving those men who had earlier declared their desire to affect the city's destiny vanished. The war grew and wilted in almost one week, with isolated skirmishes continuing over a fifteen-month period. By July 1922, Lord Justice Moore at the assizes court declared that, in relation to the city itself, he was 'very glad on the first occasion he had the honour to meet them [jurors] that he had so little to say. The city appeared to be in a quiet normal condition.'[17] This contrasts with the Co. Londonderry assize where Mr Justice Brown said that 'the total number of cases specially reported was 172, a definite increase in crime'.[18] In Derry city, because of the strength of the unionist population, both in terms of its military and financial capability as well as its geographical concentration within the city walls, no political change was forthcoming. Indeed, in February 1923, speaking at a meeting of the Londonderry Branch of the Ulster Labour Unionist Association, Councillor John Mark said that 'if Northern Ireland lost its boundary cities of Derry and Enniskillen, they would have left a portion of country, but it would lack history. The citizens of Derry were prepared to put up with anything rather than part with their ancient city or forswear their loyalty to the principles they had always held so dear.'[19] The issue of blood sacrifice was not the sole concern of Irish patriots, and considering the sacrifices made by protestants during the earlier war, it is not unusual that such sentiments were expressed. As RIC reports from earlier years stated, the majority of the protestant population in Derry city was armed and many of them put their weapons to good use during the period in question.[20] By comparison, in April 1923 the total strength of anti-Treaty IRA forces in Northern Command numbered no more than 1,170 with approximately 400 weapons – only one for every three men;[21] and the situation had been made worse for those hoping to carry the fight in the North in the aftermath of the 1921 Treaty when anti-Treaty forces in Dublin believed, particularly with reference to the Belfast Brigade, that 'it does not appear to be advisable that they should tackle the Specials at present as the Free Staters are actually informing on the Republicans'.[22] Such was the position when Unionism took centre stage in city politics once again in January 1923.

In July 1920, clauses that had been attached to the Corporation bill regarding the electoral areas had been withdrawn by the mayor; the chairman of the committee overseeing the bill in London had simply referred to the bill as 'Orange against Sinn Féin', and he could not let the bill pass unless nationalist amendments were removed and it was restored to the form given to it by the 'Orange Council', the previous corporation. The demand for electricity, which was a problem for the city's citizens and business community, was outstripping the corporation's ability to supply it – a situation that led the North of Ireland Shipbuilding Company to consider taking legal action against the corporation in 1922.[23] The city had been affected by a series of strikes throughout the period, one of which had spelt the end of Watts Distillery in 1921. The ownership of the bridge spanning the Foyle remained unresolved, and the huge expense surrounding the Banagher Water Scheme would consume future corporations with larger budgets. Indeed, one of the few major successes was the extension of street lighting and the provision of a bus service, although the latter had its critics too. Appointments to committees also exercised many corporation meetings with one in particular standing out. Unionist members greeted with displeasure the appointment of John Tracy as coroner, as he was appointed ahead of a protestant. The corporation simply voted along party lines. Alderman Richard Doherty said the position 'required independence and ability in the person filling it'. However, he continued, 'it was the only important position in the gift of the corporation that a catholic had occupied, and in consequence the new appointment should also go to a catholic'.[24] Such was the life of a corporation where religion and politics mixed. In the wider political context the operation of the corporation in relation to the new parliament in Belfast was almost unreal. In 1972, John Darby quoted the presbyterian minister and home ruler, J.M. Armour, as saying that 'having fought against home rule for almost a century Unionists were compelled to take a form of home rule that the devil himself could never have imagined. Indeed, Darby quotes the historian, J.C. Beckett, as saying that the parliament in Belfast was forced upon six counties of Ulster by London because they believed it was the only way of reconciling the two main Irish parties.[25] Derry, like other councils, simply believed that the Belfast set-up was illegal and would not be sustained. Coupled with the hope generated by the Boundary Commission, it is easy to see why the military campaign evaporated and how, by May 1925, the IRA in Dublin could look on with dismay as the military structure in Derry was more or less extinct. An IRA officer eloquently summed up the situation in 1924:

> Those of the catholic population of Ulster who supported the Treaty did so for two reasons: firstly, they were strongly influenced by the Boundary Commission Clause and secondly, they had an idea that there would be a National Government in the twenty-six counties which would safeguard them from political and economical persecutions from their own government. In both cases they have found that they have made a mistake.[26]

As moral support from Dublin evaporated through the 1920s and nationalists emerged from the 'troubled period' in a state of perpetual shock, it would be several years before their political representatives took their seats in the Northern Ireland parliament in a belated attempt to alter the status quo. In the end, with the reaffirmation of the Londonderry Improvement bill in November 1922, a 'chasm of bitterness' was reopened:

> Denied inclusion in the part of Ireland to which they gave allegiance, isolated by the nearby border from their natural and historic Donegal hinterland where so many of them had their roots, refused the municipal power to which their numbers democratically entitled them, Derry's catholics seethed with a sense of community deprivation that set the tone for future political warfare.[27]

In March, only two months after relinquishing office, Hugh C. O'Doherty died. In April, the corporation (with the exception of Nationalist members who had refused to take their seats) passed a motion remembering his contribution to the city's affairs:

> We, the Mayor, Aldermen and Burgesses of the City of Londonderry, in Common Council assembled, hereby place on record our sense of the extreme loss the community has suffered in the sad and untimely death of Mr Hugh C. O'Doherty, ex-mayor of this City, who, by his firmness, courage and impartiality during the difficult period he occupied the Mayoral Chair saved the Citizens and the City from much of the strife and disaster which overtook the rest of the country. We desire further to express our deep sympathy with his widow and family in the sad blow which has fallen upon them, and let the Town Clerk forward a copy of this resolution to Mrs Doherty.[28]

Although the city saw many deaths in 1920, O'Doherty, by refusing to use his people as sacrificial lambs at the altar of 'republican principle', saved the city and citizens from bitter internal strife. However, the division of the country and the exclusion of Derry from the Free State only clouded the issue of sovereignty for another day. The corporation's action simply ensured that the problem would be inherited by future generations. That it took another forty-five years to resurface, and erupted with the same ferocity that marked a few fleeting weeks in 1920, may have surprised many people, but O'Doherty's stance had merely delayed the inevitable.

Appendix

List of aldermen and councillors for Derry corporation

Political affiliations, which were pencilled in the margin of the document, are indicated as follows: Nationalist (N); Unionist (U), and Sinn Féin (SF). The 'L' denotes those that Dublin believed to have labour/socialist interests. Source: NA, DELG 18/11.

ALDERMEN

Hugh C. O'Doherty — Mayor, Independent (previously aligned to the Irish Parliamentary Party)

Humphrey Babington	U	Alexander Anderson	U
James Bonner	N	Charles (Cathal) Bradley	SF
Thomas Bible	U	Patrick Meenan	N
James Ballatine	U	Conn Bradley	SF
Richard Doherty	N		

COUNCILLORS

William Bradley	N	Sir John McFarland	U
John Burns	U	H.S. Robinson	U
Michael Cosgrove	SF	W.H. Elliot	U
James Hamilton	U	James Blair	U
Con Doherty	N	J.H. Pollock	U
H. Crawford McCay	U	Margaret Morris	SF
James Gallagher	SF (L)	Anthony Carlin	SF
J.G. Magee	U	Patrick Hegarty	SF
Robert McAnaney	SF (L)	William Logue	N (L)
R.A. Deane	U	Joseph McClean	N
Edward McCafferty	SF (L)	Joseph McKernan	N
Daniel O'Donnell	N	Dominick J. Shiel	SF*
R.K. Gilliland	U	D.P. Thompson	U
H.H. Greenway	U (L)	Thomas McCully	U
S. Wallace Kennedy	U	Florence O'Sullivan	N

*This should read *Patrick Shiels*.

Notes

ABBREVIATIONS

DJ	*Derry Journal*
LCM	Londonderry Corporation Minutes
II	*Irish Independent*
IN	*Irish News*
IT	*Irish Times*
LG	*Londonderry Guardian*
LN	*Londonderry Newsletter*
LS	*Londonderry Standard*
NLI	National Library of Ireland, Dublin
MA	Military Archives, Dublin
PRONI	Public Record Office of Northern Ireland
UCDA	University College Dublin Archives

1. BACKGROUND: SETTING THE SCENE FOR 1920

1 E. Moloney, *A secret history of the IRA* (London, 2002), p. 535.
2 J. Hume, 'Social and economic aspects of the growth of Derry 1825–1850' (unpublished MA thesis, Maynooth, 1964). A book based on Mr Hume's thesis was published in 2002 by the Ulster Historical Foundation.
3 *LG*, 22 July 1869.
4 Frank Curran, *Derry: countdown to disaster* (Dublin, 1986), p. 5.
5 Knox received 2,033 votes to the Unionist John Ross' 1,994. Unionism regained the seat in 1892 but subsequently lost it again in 1895, before a Unionist was returned in 1900.
6 Curran, op. cit., p. 6. The architect of these successive schemes was the town clerk, Sir Henry Miller.
7 The duke of Abercorn held the seat until his death on 3 January: Hogg defeated Colonel Pakenham by a majority of 57 seats.
8 Tillie was a shirt-manufacturer: 1,300 of his 1,500 employees were Roman Catholic. He refused to sign the Ulster Covenant 'as home rule was the democratic decision of the people of the UK'.
9 D. Murphy, *Derry, Donegal and modern Ulster, 1790–1921* (Derry, 1979) p. 180.
10 M. Laffan, *The partition of Ireland, 1911–25* (Dundalk, 1986), p. 9.
11 M. Bradley, 'Bishop McHugh of Derry' unpublished B.A. thesis, Maynooth College, 1985, p. 15.
12 Mary Gallagher remembers her father speaking about his brothers joining too. They attended meetings in the local parish hall addressed by the parish priest in 1914, where they were encouraged to join and fight for Belgium and home rule.
13 Eoin MacNeill attended one such rally in September 1917.
14 Lacy, op. cit., p. 223.
15 E. Daly, *The clergy of the diocese of Derry* (Dublin, 1997), p. 103. A native of Donaghmore, McGlinchey was an ardent nationalist and promoter of the Irish language.
16 Derry Journal [*DJ*], 4 Jan. 1918.
17 *DJ*, 4 Jan. 1918.
18 *DJ*, 11 Feb. 1918.
19 Bradley, 'Bishop McHugh', p. 17.
20 *DJ*, 10 Apr. 1918.
21 *DJ*, 24 June 1918.
22 See Jérôme ann de Wiel's '"The Hay Plan": an account of Anglo-French recruitment efforts in Ireland, August 1918', in *Irish Sword* 21, no. 86 (1999) 434–45.
23 E. Phoenix, *Northern nationalism: nationalist politics, partition and the catholic minority in Northern Ireland, 1890–1940* (Belfast, 1994), pp 49–56.
24 *DJ*, 25 Nov. 1918.
25 See issues of the *Derry Journal* in October and November 1918 for such evidence
26 Charles Diamond was another benefactor. Formerly a member o[f] the Irish Party, he was now controller of *London Catholic Herald* and the *Glasgow Observer.* He donated £250 to Sinn Féin o[f] which £83 went to MacNeill's Derry campaign.
27 *DJ*, 13 Dec. 1918.
28 *DJ*, 30 Dec. 1918.
29 MacNeill received 7,455 votes as opposed to 7,020 for the Unionis[t] candidate.
30 *DJ*, 30 Dec. 1918.

2. THE LOCAL ELECTION 1920

1 *DJ*, 21 Jan. 1919.
2 *DJ*, 14 July 1919.
3 *DJ*, 21 July 1919.
4 *DJ*, 13 Aug. 1919.
5 *DJ*, 18 Sept. 1919.
6 Ibid.
7 *Proportional representation illustrated and explained: application to local government elections* (Belfast, 1919), p. 8.
8 As harbour commissioner, Charles O'Neill opposed partition in his submission to the Boundary Commission in 1925 (PRONI, D/868/4).
9 *DJ*, 15 Sept. 1919.
10 *DJ*, 15 Dec. 1919.
11 Colm Fox, *The making of a minority: political developments in Derry and the north, 1912–25* (Derry, 1997), pp 68–9.
12 *DJ*, 16 Jan. 1920.
13 The *Journal* alleged that John Glendenning (president), Robert Watson, and Fannie Corscaden, who were all prominent unionists in the city's business community, signed the letter.
14 *DJ*, 14 Jan. 1920.
15 *DJ*, 16 Jan. 1920, both sides 'had a good supply of vehicles, including a large fleet of motor cars, at their disposal'.
16 Ibid, 'A lady octogenarian who was unable either to see or use her limbs spiritedly appeared on the scene in a bath chair, and was borne, seated down on the chair, to the top of the stairs on the shoulders of four supporters'.
17 Ibid.
18 *DJ*, 21 Jan. 1920.
19 *LS*, 22 Jan. 1920.
20 *DJ*, 21 Jan. 1920.
21 Ibid.
22 *IN*, 19 Jan. 1920.
23 *DJ*, 2 Feb. 1920.
24 Anderson had stepped down as mayor in Dec. 1919 allegedly on grounds of ill health.
25 *DJ*, 2 Feb. 1920.
26 Ibid.
27 A comprehensive account of O'Doherty's speech is given in *DJ*, 2 Feb. 1920.

3. THE FIGHT FOR INDEPENDENCE

1 B. Mac Giolla Chiolle (ed.), *Intelligence Notes*, 1913–16: *Chief Secretary's Office, Dublin Castle*, (Dublin, 1966), p. 203. The Irish Volunteers were formed as a result of a split from the National Volunteers over Redmond's war policies.
2 Ibid., p. 25.
3 *DJ*, 9 Feb. 1920.
4 They were J.P. McKinley, Eamonn McDermott, and Patrick Shiels.
5 Criminal Injuries Register (PRONI, Lond/6/3/1/2).
6 *DJ*, 15 Mar. 1920.
7 Ibid.
8 The *Journal* quoted an unnamed source as saying that the threat to the mayor was in the form of a letter: 'in the event of a policeman being murdered in Co. Wexford he should prepare to meet his end': 24 Mar. 1920.
9 *DJ*, 2 Apr. 1920.
10 The Laird liner *Rose* was searched on 3 April and weapons were found.
11 *DJ*, 16 Apr. 1920: 'the religion of the employees was the determining factor as to whether they joined in or not'.
12 *DJ*, 19 Apr. 1920.
13 Augusteijn, 'Radical nationalist activities in Co. Derry 1900–1921' in G. O'Brien (ed.), *Derry and Londonderry: history and society* (Dublin, 1999). pp 573–600.
14 *DJ*, 7 May 1920.
15 Ibid., 14 May 1920.
16 Ibid.
17 Moroney was buried in Hollymount, Co. Mayo, with his wife. However, his immediate family were not happy with this and his body was exhumed and driven to Clare 'where it was re-interred in the burial ground of his own people'.
18 *DJ*, 17 May 1920.
19 Ibid.
20 *DJ*, 19 May 1920.
21 E. Phoenix, *Northern nationalism*, p. 87.
22 Forbesm Patterson was a Presbyterian nationalist from Ballintoy in Co. Antrim. He was editor of *Red Hand*, a Belfast Sinn Féin journal founded by F.J. Bigger in 1920.
23 Ó hEigceartuigh to Collins, 29 Apr. 1920 (NA, DE/2/89).
24 Michael Collins, *Path to freedom* (Dublin, 1922); 'I think we shall safely avoid State Socialism, which has nothing to commend it in a country like Ireland', p. 133.
25 *DJ*, 21 May 1920.
26 Charles Townshend, 'The Irish railway strike of 1920: industrial action and civil resistance in the struggle for independence', in *Irish Historical Studies* 21, no. 83 (1979) 265–82.
27 See *LS* and *DS* week beginning 31 May.
28 Eamon Phoenix, *Northern nationalism*, quotes from police files alleging that the violence was 'sudden', p. 87.
29 *DJ*, 16 May 1920.
30 See page 28 for additional details.
31 Statement regarding riots in Derry in June 1920 (NLI, Kathleen McKenna Napoli papers, MS 22743).
32 *DJ*, 15 May 1953, article by Liam A. Brady.
33 The republican activist, Countess Markievicz, set up Fianna Éireann as a militant nationalist boy scout organization in 1911. During Easter 1916, its members ferried arms and supplies across Dublin.
34 *DS*, 21 June 1920.
35 *DJ*, 15 May 1953.
36 *II*, 22 June 1920.
37 *DJ*, 15 June 1953.
38 *DJ*, 23 June 1920.
39 Ibid.
40 *DS*, 25 June 1920, Colonel Perry Williams and Colonel Gretton were quoted as accusing the Government of allowing soldiers to stand idly by while the warring factions fought in Derry.
41 *DJ*, 25 June 1920.
42 Sherrin to Michael Collins (MA, Collins papers, A0464).
43 *DJ*, 25 June 1920.
44 *DJ*, 28 June 1920.
45 *DJ*, 30 June 1920.
46 Ibid.: 'it is to be regretted that they did nothing to protect the premises of a catholic, Mr Fred O'Hanlon, whose private house next door to the Post Office was looted, furniture and fittings being smashed and clothing carried away': the men arrested were William Kane, Samuel King, Thomas Gamble, Samuel Fleming, John Lappin, Samuel Robb, James Logan, John Lorimer, and William Wilson.
47 *DJ*, 15 June 1953.
48 *DJ*, 2 July 1920.
49 A Belfast court eventually found Gray not guilty. However, the *Journal* noted on 6 Jan. 1922 his subsequent death. It reminded readers that O'Kane, before dying, had said to his brother, 'I was shot by Gray, of Benvarden Avenue, the fellow with the one arm'.
50 LCM, July 1920; *DJ*, 7 July 1920.
51 Statement of Northern situation (UCDA, Michael Hayes papers, P53/172). Hayes had fought at Jacob's factory in 1916 before being elected in 1918 one of four TDs

representing the National University. He held ministries in successive governments post-1922 before being called to the Bar in 1929. He finished his career as a university professor.

52 *DJ*, 9 July 1920.
53 See *LS* and *DJ*, 23 July 1920.
54 Of 63,354 legal permits to hold weapons in Ireland, only 298 were in Derry.
55 Smyth, a divisional commissioner with the RIC, was killed on 17 July in Cork city. Although born in India, his parents came from Ulster. It was believed in Ulster that he was chosen because he was a protestant. At the time, however, he had been advocating the killing of 'Sinn Féiners' to solve the Irish problem. See T. P. Coogan's *Michael Collins: a biography* (London, 1990), pp 150–3.
56 *DJ*, 26 July 1920.
57 See *DJ*, 20 May 1953 for Liam Brady's article regarding the period.
58 *An t-Óglach*, 1 Sept. 1920.
59 The authorities attributed the attack on the RIC barracks to James Moore, 27 Nelson Street (PRONI, HA/5/2328).
60 Swanzy had been transferred from Cork in the aftermath of MacCurtain's killing.
61 Witness accounts about such incidents recorded in Hayes' papers (UCDA, Michael Hayes papers, P53/150–160).
62 Glass was found not guilty on 20 Aug. (PRONI, Crown & Peace Files, Lond1/2/3/21).
63 *DJ*, 30 Aug. 1920.
64 *DJ*, 27 Sept. 1920.
65 Francis Wright was subsequently charged with O'Hara's shooting but found not guilty; the assizes noted that 'the accused had a large number of people as defence witnesses' (PRONI, Crown & Peace files, Lond1/3/2/21).
66 See *LS*, 18 Oct. & *DJ*, 20 Oct. 1920.
67 See J. Herlihy, *The Royal Irish Constabulary: a short history and genealogical guide* (Dublin, 1997), for a listing of police casualties during the period. It seems almost that Flaherty was shot by loyalists.
68 Brady incorrectly dates this event as 8 November.
69 See *DJ* 20 May 1953 for Liam Brady's account of this event.
70 Michael Farrell, *Northern Ireland: the Orange State* (London, 1976), pp 34–6.
71 Herlihy, *Royal Irish Constabulary*, p. 192; policemen's service records in author's possession.
72 *DJ*, 9 Feb. 1921: Heneghan was from Mayo, and along with a school friend, Michael Burke, joined the RIC on 16 Dec. 1912 and was posted with Burke to Derry on 28 June 1913. (Even their serial numbers followed on from each other.) The IRA killed Burke during an attack in the town of Swatragh in June 1921. A Derry-man, John McDaid, from Creggan Road, was later charged with the killing.
73 *DJ*, 18 May 1953 & Augusteijn, 'Radical nationalist activities', p. 585.
74 Derry's district commandant was S. Wallace Kennedy.
75 *DJ*, 1 Nov. 1920: subsequent events would prove that they were a law unto themselves.
76 Clancy & McKee went to Derry in June 1920 as military advisors (MA, Collins Papers, A0464).
77 See E. O'Connor, *A labour history of Ireland, 1824–1960* (Dublin, 1992).
78 A. Bielenberg, 'The Watt family and the distilling industry in Derry 1762–1921', *Ulster Folklife* 11 (1994) 1–11.
79 *DJ*, 29 Nov. 1920.
80 Telegraph lines were cut in January, April and June (PRONI, Criminal Registers, Lond6/3/1/2).
81 McGuinness, a flamboyant character at the best of times, wrote about his life in a book called *Nomad*. He was constantly under surveillance and it was noted in RIC reports that he openly brandished a revolver while wearing an IRA officer's uniform. The RIC in Belfast noted that he was 'the man wanted for the murder of Inspector Johnston at Glasgow and had escaped from Ebrington Barracks': 18 Oct. 1921 (NLI, P8561, Box 154 634/772).
82 See Bill Kelly (ed.), *Sworn to be free, the complete book of IRA jailbreaks, 1918–1921* (Tralee, 1971). Oscar Norby had been helping the IRA since early 1920 and had brought in gelignite and weapons that were used nationwide by the IRA.
83 *DJ*, 26 Jan. 1921.
84 Phoenix, *Northern nationalism*, p. 91.
85 Those boycotted in Derry were: S.M. Kennedy, drapery and shirt factory owner; Mr English, Millar & Beattie's; W.G. McLoughlin, shirt factory; Derry Hosiery Company (R.A. Anderson); Derry Barrell Company; Mark, Rouston & McLaughlin Pork Curers (NA, DE4/9/1).
86 Augusteijn, op. cit., p. 583.
87 *DJ*, 7 Feb. 1921.
88 See *Sentinel, Standard and Journal*, 2–5 Apr. 1921.
89 Augusteijn, op cit, p. 592.
90 *DJ*, 3 June 1953: Brady alleged that a plan was devised to blow up the bridge but was aborted when the Truce was announced in July 1921.
91 Augusteijn, 'Radical nationalist activities', p. 589.
92 *DJ*, 11 Apr. 1921.
93 Ibid., 25 Apr. 1921 & 4 May 1921.
94 The anti-partitionist vote was 23,658, of which 15,886 went to Eoin MacNeill, the SF candidate. George Leeke, a local hotelier, secured the other seat for the combined nationalist front.
95 *DJ*, 15 Aug. 1921.
96 T.P. Coogan, *Michael Collins*, pp 342–47: the border area remained tense when the *Journal* reported (13 Feb. 1922) on the Clones Railway Station affair. Free State troops shot dead four 'Specials' after Matthew Fitzpatrick, the IRA commandant of the detachment, was killed. One of the 'Specials' was a Derryman called William J. Doherty, from Florence Street.
97 *DJ*, 7 Dec. 1921.
98 PRONI, HA/5/600: see *DJ* 17 Feb. 1922 & 24 July 1922.
99 Whether the latter person was actually Lieutenant M. Sherrin, who reported to Collins, is debatable.
100 Letter from Mr Laurenson to Mr Bunting, 29 Sept. 1922 (PRONI, HA/8/38/31).
101 See D. Harkness, *Northern Ireland since 1920* (Dublin, 1986), M. Laffan, *The resurrection of Ireland: the Sinn Féin party, 1916–23* (Cambridge, 1999), and Farrell, *Northern Ireland*.
102 Intelligence Dept., 1st Northern Division to Shiels, 2 Feb. 1922 (PRONI, CAB6/35). A copy of the letter in CAB/HA5 had been removed and marked 'disclose 2005'
103 *DJ*, 24 May 1922.
104 Patrick Shiels moved to Donegal after Twaddell's killing. P. Cahill, district inspector, writing in Sept. said that 'the real reason he

cleared out was because he was afraid he would be shot by the Special Constabulary as a reprisal for Mr Twaddell's murder' (PRONI, HA/5/2164).

05 Within one week of the USC constables being killed, five catholics were shot in Co. Derry, three of them dead.

06 D. Kleinrichert, *Republican internment and the prison ship Argenta* (Dublin, 2001), pp 26–31.

07 Horner was a captain in the IRA; his sister, N.S. Horner, worked in Dublin Castle (NLI, Dublin Castle Records, P8561 Box 154, 904/790)

08 For extensive coverage see *Sentinel, Standard* and *Journal* week beginning 23 May.

09 Horner was originally from Fermanagh but lived in Derry. On his release in Dec. 1923, he was permitted to stay in Derry for five days – to see his family – before leaving for the Free State. The condition of his release was his expulsion from the Six Counties. He subsequently joined the Free State army (PRONI, HA/5/1605).

10 *DJ*, 25 Apr. 1922.

11 Secret departmental memo, 22 June 1922 (PRONI, HA/32/1/194).

12 Sally-Flood to Ministry for Home Affairs, 29 June 1922 (PRONI, HA/32/1/194).

13 Secret departmental memo, 22 July 1922 (PRONI, HA/32/1/194).

14 *DJ*, 12 July 1922.

15 *DJ*, 8 Sept. 1922.

16 Woods to Richard Mulcahy, 21 Sept. 1922 (UCDA, Mulcahy papers, P7/B/287).

17 See *DJ*, 29 Sept. 1922, for report on corporation business. McAnaney suffered the tragic loss of a daughter when she was accidentally shot by a Free State soldier in Burnfoot in June. See *DJ*, 2 June 1922.

18 General Headquarters to all Commands, 7 Dec. 1922 (NLI, James O'Donovan papers, MS 22301).

19 O'Donovan to unidentified person, 28 Feb. 22 (NLI, James O'Donovan papers, MS 22301).

20 The use of 'Londonderry' by the *Sentinel* is interesting. In many PRONI files (government and non-government) consulted by the author, the city was frequently referred to as 'Derry'.

21 *LS*, 13 Feb. 1923.

22 Key members of this Company were: district commander: Alderman Mark; sub-commanders: Mr W. J. Hepburn, No. 1 Company; Samuel Heatley, No. 2 Company; Captain H. McKee, No. 3 Company; Joseph Wallace, No. 4 Company; William Thomas, No. 5 Company; W. J. Hyndman, adjutant of battalion; Caldwell Kennedy; and Sergeant William McGahey.

4. THE CORPORATION

1 Farrell, op. cit., p. 25.

2 Ministry of Commerce report on economic dependence of Londonderry, 29 Sept. 1923 (PRONI, CAB/8/F/14).

3 See W. Kelly (ed.), *The sieges of Derry* (Dublin, 2001).

4 *DJ*, 2 Feb. 1920.

5 See page 00 for coverage of his speech.

6 *DJ*, 2 Feb. 1920.

7 *DJ*, 15 Mar. 1920: Alderman Babington KC, a local unionist, supported the mayor on this issue.

8 LCM, 16 Mar. 1920.

9 Ibid., 16 Mar. 1920. See also *DJ*, 17 Mar. & *LS*, 18 Mar. 1920 for reports on meeting.

10 *DJ*, 21 Apr. 1920.

11 *DJ*, 21 Apr. 1920; LCM, Apr. 1920.

12 LCM, Apr. 1920.

13 *DJ*, 23 June 1920.

14 Ibid.

15 See page 28 concerning code words for a liaison between the British army and UVF.

16 Unionists missing on 21 June were: James Ballatine; Alexander Anderson; John Burns; James Hamilton; R.K. Gilliland; S. Wallace Kennedy; Sir John McFarland; H.S. Robinson; James Blair; Thomas McCully; Humphrey Babington; Thomas Bible.

17 LCM, 21 June 1920.

18 *DJ*, 23 July 1920.

19 LCM, 15 Mar. 1920.

20 Letter to Secretary, Sinn Féin from Patrick Shiels, 22 Aug. 1920 (NA, DELG 18/11). Alderman Cathal Bradley was with the mayor when they met with Griffith.

21 Ibid., 22 Aug. 1920 (NA, DELG 18/11).

22 Letter to Secretary, Sinn Féin, from Patrick Shiels, 24 Aug. 1920 (NA, DELG 18/11).

23 Unsigned letter to Local Government Ministry, 25 Sept. 1920 (NA, DELG 18/11).

24 Referring to the proposed new Education bill, McHugh remarked in his pastoral letter of Feb. 1920: 'a bureaucratic Body, composed of two Scotchmen and a Government official, is to be set up to control the religious and secular education of Ireland'.

25 *DJ*, 18 Oct. 1920.

26 *DJ*, 10 Nov. 1920.

27 'It is admitted by Unionists in Derry that the new control has shown both zeal and ability – has done its work creditably. It is admitted by Sinn Féiners that the Unionist officials have been perfectly loyal to their new masters and have given them all assistance. It is known further by the general community that Sinn Féin has not used its advantage in a provocative manner': quoted in *DJ*, 23 June 1920.

28 *DJ*, 26 Jan. 1921.

29 *DJ*, 17 Jan. 1921.

30 *DJ*, 19 Jan. 1921.

31 Much to the disgust of local businessmen (like R.P. Hogg) Dublin suppliers increased coal prices in April.

32 LCM, Apr. 1921.

33 Collins to de Valera, 15 Jan. 1921 (NA, DE 2/266): handwritten at the top of the page were the words 'Letter by Michael Collins to President Arthur Griffith (scored out) de Valera'.

34 Total anti-partitionist vote was 23,658, of which 15,886 went to Eoin MacNeill, the SF candidate. George Leeke, a local hotelier, secured the other seat for the combined nationalist front.

35 The Shankill Road was a working-class protestant area in Belfast.

36 Bielenberg, op. cit., p. 9.

37 LCM, Aug. 1920. In attendance were: Aldermen Richard Doherty, Bonner, Cathal Bradley, Con Bradley, Babington, Anderson; Councillors Mrs Morris, Logue, McKernan, McCafferty, Gallagher, Sheil, O'Donnell, McAnaney, Con Doherty, McClean, Hegarty, O'Sullivan, Cosgrove, Burns, Thompson, Hamilton, McCay, Blair, Greenway, Deane, McFarland, Elliott, Magee, Pollock, Kennedy, and Mark.

38 This was almost a tacit admittance by Burns that unionist councillors were partly to blame for rioting in June 1920; something Alderman Meenan accused them of at a corporation meeting on 21 June 1920.

39 *DJ*, 26 Aug. 1921.

40 *DJ*, 14 Sept. 1921: in the deputation were Alderman Cathal

Bradley, Councillors McAnaney, Shiels and P.J. Hegarty; Mr John Leonard, J. McLaughlin & H. O'Doherty were represented the GAA.

41 Phoenix, *Northern nationalism*, pp 145–9.

42 The *Journal* reported (9 Dec.) under the headline 'sensational development' that de Valera had rejected the terms of the Treaty.

43 The Derry city and county contingent of the delegation was: Derry delegates: Edward Logue (Dungiven); William Mullan (Claudy); John McHenry (Feeny); P. Lynch (Park); Francis Kelly (Magherafelt); Seamus O'Craimis (Derry); Domnac Ui Siaduil (Derry); W. Doherty (Derry city); Jas Gallagher (Derry), (NA, DE 4/9/44).

44 See John Bowman, *De Valera and the Ulster question, 1917–73* (Oxford, 1982).

45 Letter to mayor of Derry and town clerk from P. Shiels, P. Hegarty, Cathal Bradley, Anthony Carlin, Michael Cosgrove, 22 Dec. 1921 (NLI, Eoin MacNeill papers, MS 10881).

46 Bishop McHugh to MacNeill, 26 Dec. 1921 (NLI, Eoin MacNeill papers, MS 10881).

47 For his concerns for the Academy at this juncture in Dec., see his correspondence (NLI, Eoin MacNeill papers, MS 10880).

48 *DJ*, 6 Jan. 1922.

49 LCM, 10 Jan. 1922.

50 *DJ*, 27 Jan. 1922.

51 *DJ*, 10 Apr. 1922.

52 *DJ*, 5 Apr. 1922.

53 *DJ*, 29 May 1922.

54 The North of Ireland Shipbuilding Company sought the advice of E.S. Murphy KC on whether or not they had grounds to sue the corporation as a result of the closure. However, he concluded: 'I cannot, however, find in any of the documents any indication of any contract on the part of the corporation to complete the extension of their power station within a definitive period' (PRONI, D/1326/18/30).

55 See *LS*, 22 July 1922, & *DS*, 21 July 1922: the reference to the McMahons concerned a family in Belfast that had been killed in March; at the time it was alleged the Ulster Special Constabulary carried out the killings. Eamon Phoenix revisited this accusation in an article in *IN*, 5 Mar. 2001.

56 Phoenix, op. cit., p. 233.

57 Margaret O'Callaghan, 'Old parchment and water: the Boundary Commission of 1925 and the copperfastening of the Irish border' in *Bullán* 4, no. 2 (winter 1999/spring 2000) 27–55.

58 Margaret O'Doherty was the wife of Joseph O'Doherty, a Sinn Féin TD for Donegal.

59 In May 1973 Dr. Raymond McClean, a member of the Social and Democratic Labour Party (SDLP), became the first nationalist mayor since O'Doherty.

CONCLUSION

1 As quoted in the *LS*, 4 Jan. 1923.

2 *DJ*, 24 Jan. 1923.

3 LCM, 18 Dec. 1922.

4 Phoenix, *Northern nationalism*, pp 161–6.

5 *DJ*, 31 May 1922.

6 *DJ*, 26 May 1922.

7 The killings in May 1922 in Desertmartin, Co. Derry, illustrated the capacity of the USC for retaliatory action (see UCDA, Michael Hayes papers, P53/181); see also *DJ*, 22 May 1922.

8 A district inspector referred to 1920–23 as 'the troubled period' when discussing the transfer of RUC HQ from Derry to Coleraine in 1927 (PRONI, HA/4/1/194).

9 *IN*, 16 Feb. 2001.

10 'Memorandum on the Northern Question' (incomplete), *c.*May 1922; McKenna was a secretary to the Ministry for Propaganda and, according to Joost Augusteijn, 'is a reliable witness' (NLI, McKenna Napoli papers, MS 22780).

11 Letter to Aitken from Patrick Hurd regarding the transfer of arms to Ulster in June 1922: 'we brought these rifles to Drumboe Castle and from there we took them in small quantities to the Border and smuggled them into the Six Counties', 19 Nov. 1927 (UCDA, Frank Aitken papers, P104/1261).

12 Coogan, *Michael Collins*, p. 340.

13 Some of the items that exercised Dublin during the period were: the purchase of a painting for Dublin corporation; the promotion of Irish books via the Indian Revolutionary Committee; and the allocation of money for a Dante celebration.

14 See Irish National Academy under Professor Corcoran, 22 Feb. 1922 (NA, DE/Ministry & Cabinet Minutes).

15 PRONI, D/1326/18/30.

16 Lt Sherrin to Collins, July 1920 (MA, Collins Papers, A0464).

17 *DJ*, 26 July 1922.

18 *DJ*, 24 July 1922.

19 *LS*, 13 Feb. 1923.

20 When retiring from the 'Specials' in November 1968, J.M. Harvey, a colleague of Alderman McFarland in the Londonderry Unionist Association and member of the USC in the 1920s, returned the following weaponry: revolver with Unicorn butt, .500 Rigby Revolver, 41 calibre Colt, Mauser Revolver (no. 95686) in wooden box, .303 rifle, BSA .22 rifle, Lee Enfield, John Neill Mark Tower 1866 below cocking piece, Olympic model .22, .303 SMLE Mark III rifle; more than likely the Mauser rifle was part of a consignment of weapons landed by the UVF in Larne in 1914 (PRONI, Harvey papers, D/3054/4).

21 Memo to anti-Treaty IRA HQ, Dublin 15 Mar. 1923 (UCDA, Moss Twomey papers, P69/35/259

22 Department memo, Mar. 1923 (UCDA, Moss Twomey papers, P69/35/286).

23 See North of Ireland Shipbuilding Company files (PRONI, D/1326/18/30).

24 *Derry Journal*, 28 July 1920; see also LCM, 27 June 1920.

25 John Darby (ed.), *Northern Ireland: the background to the conflict* (Belfast 1983), pp 11, 20.

26 Unsigned memo from Belfast to anti-Treaty IRA HQ, 16 Apr. 192[illegible] (UCDA, Moss Twomey papers, P69/36/161).

27 Curran, *Derry*, p. 9.

28 Motion was proposed by the mayor and seconded by Alderman Sir John McFarland, 4 Apr. 1923.